OLE MISS

DAILY DEVOTIONS FOR DIE-HARD FANS

REBELS

OLE MISS

Daily Devotions for Die-Hard Fans: Ole Miss Rebels
© 2011 Ed McMinn
Extra Point Publishers; P.O. Box 871; Perry GA 31069

Library of Congress Cataloging-in-Publication Data
13 ISBN Digit ISBN: 978-0-9846377-2-0

Manufactured in the United States of America.

Go to http://www.die-hardfans.com for information about other titles in
the series.

Cover and interior design by Slynn McMinn.

REBELS

Dedicated to the Glory of God

Author's Note: *The name "Ole Miss" did not appear until 1896, three years after the beginning of the football program, and the school's athletic teams were not designated as the "Rebels" until 1936. For simplicity's sake, I have used the two terms throughout the book to refer to the University and its athletic teams respectively.*

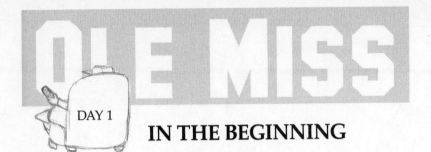

IN THE BEGINNING

Read Genesis 1, 2:1-3.

"God saw all that he had made, and it was very good" (v. 1:31).

On Nov. 11, 1893, a group of young Baptists piled off a train and was promptly engulfed by "a sea of shouting and laughing Mississippians." Football at Ole Miss had begun.

For six weeks, a young Latin and Greek professor, Dr. Alexander Bondurant, had been putting sixteen students through some grueling practices in an effort to shape them into the university's first football team. He drilled them twice a day on the game's fundamentals. He also fed them healthful meals at a training table and had them sign a pledge to "abstain from tobacco, coffee, tea and all intoxicants" and to abide by a 10 p.m. curfew.

As the first-ever game day neared, the newly formed Athletic Association and some Oxford citizens who passed the hat purchased "uniforms of a cheap kind." The players furnished their own shoes and agreed to be responsible for any medical expenses incurred as a result of injuries. Bondurant established Harvard red and Yale blue as the team colors, declaring "it was well to have the spirit of both these good colleges."

The first-ever opponent was Southwestern Baptist University. An exuberant crowd met the team at the Oxford train station with a hearty welcome and escorted the visitors around town in horse-drawn carriages. Players from both teams sat around downtown

REBELS

for a while and convivially talked things over.

From the start of the 3 p.m. kickoff, the game belonged to the local lads. History records that Mordecai Jones, a halfback and senior law student from Newnan, Ga., scored the first touchdown in Ole Miss football history. Mississippi won 56-0.

"Every man did his duty, and for an opening game the performance was rather unusual," Bondurant later wrote about the beginning of football at Ole Miss.

Beginnings are important, but what we make of them is even more important. Consider, for example, how far the Ole Miss football program has come since that first afternoon in 1893.

Every morning of your life, you get a gift from God: a new beginning. God hands to you as an expression of divine love a new day full of promise and the chance to right the wrongs in your life. You can use the day to pay a debt, start a new relationship, replace a burned-out light bulb, tell your family you love them, chase a dream, solve a nagging problem . . . or not.

God simply provides the gift. How you use it is up to you. People often talk wistfully about starting over or making a new beginning. God gives you the chance with the dawning of every new day. You have the chance today to make things right – and that includes your relationship with God.

[Beginning the football program] was a courageous undertaking, for there was not a man in the student body who had ever played the game.
-- Dr. Alexander L. Bondurant

Every day is not just a dawn; it is a precious
chance to start over or begin anew.

DAY 2

STRANGE BUT TRUE

Read Isaiah 55.

"My thoughts are not your thoughts, neither are your ways my way" (v. 8).

Strange as it may sound, Ole Miss once had a game that was decided by a field goal that was good -- and then no good.

The 1983 Egg Bowl featured what is perhaps the strangest comeback in the series' long and storied history. It was a game that Mississippi State dominated for three quarters but didn't win, thanks in part to what was termed the "Immaculate Deflection."

State led 23-7 as the third quarter wound down, but on the last play the Bulldogs fumbled at their own 12. On the first play of the fourth quarter, the Rebs returned the favor, but the ball bounced backward right into the hands of quarterback Kelly Powell, who jogged in for a touchdown.

Three plays later, the flummoxed Bulldogs fumbled again, and defensive end Matthew Lovelady claimed it for Ole Miss at the State 22. Powell hit receiver Tim Moffett -- who in the first half had returned a punt 66 yards for a touchdown -- with a 10-yard TD pass. Suddenly, the score was 23-21.

Two plays after the kickoff, safety Joe Hall intercepted a pass at the MSU 18. This time, the Rebs couldn't punch it in, but sophomore Neil Teevan was true on a 35-yard field goal. Ole Miss led 24-23 in one of the strangest 17-point comebacks in football history: The Rebs had scored 17 points in five and one-half minutes despite running only thirteen plays and covering only 52 yards.

But that wasn't nearly as strange as the finish. With 24 seconds left, the Bulldogs attempted a 27-yard field goal. "It went straight and long and over (?) the crossbar, and State fans went wild." Just as the ball reached its zenith, however, a sudden 40 mph gust of wind incredibly pushed the ball back. It landed "a good 10 yards shy of its intended destination. Rebel fans went bananas."

Life is just strange, isn't it? How else to explain the college bowl situation, Dr. Phil, tattoos, curling, tofu, and teenagers? Isn't it strange that today we have more ways to stay in touch with each other yet are losing the intimacy of personal contact?

And how strange is God's plan to save us? Think a minute about what God did. He could have come roaring down, destroying and blasting everyone whose sinfulness offended him, which, of course, is pretty much all of us. Then he could have brushed off his hands, nodded the divine head, and left a scorched planet in his wake. All in a day's work.

Instead, God came up with a totally novel plan: He would save the world by becoming a human being, letting himself be humiliated, tortured, and killed, and thus establishing a kingdom of justice and righteousness that will last forever.

We certainly wouldn't have done it that way -- but thanks be to God that his ways are not our ways.

It is probably the only field goal ever celebrated by both teams.
-- Ole Miss' Langston Rogers on 1983's Immaculate Deflection

It's strange but true: God allowed himself
to be killed on a cross to save the world.

DAY 3

GROWING PAINS

Read Mark 4:21-32.

"'[The kingdom of God] is like a mustard seed, which is the smallest seed you plant in the ground. Yet when planted, it grows and becomes the largest of all garden plants'" (vv. 31-32).

The opportunity for growth was why Todd Abernethy chose to play basketball for Ole Miss. The growth just had nothing to do with what happened on the court.

Abernethy finished his career in Oxford with the 2006-07 season in which he averaged 11.2 points and 5.5 assists per game. A 6-1 point guard, he led the team in assists his last three seasons. He is sixth all-time in the Ole Miss record book with 158 career threes and was the thirty-first player in school history to score more than 1,000 points in a career. He made the All-SEC freshman team and was the SEC Sixth Man of the Year as a sophomore.

Abernethy and Ole Miss head coach Rod Barnes connected instantly during one phone call that virtually wrapped up a commitment though Abernethy knew nothing about Oxford and the coach had never seen him play. What they shared, they discovered, was a deep, abiding relationship with Jesus Christ.

From basketball-crazy Indiana, Abernethy finished his career as his high school's all-time leading scorer. His father is Tom Abernethy, a member of the undefeated national champions at Indiana. But for Todd, the game was always second to his faith.

REBELS

So, when he seriously began searching for a college, he looked for a place that would let him grow not just as a basketball player but especially in his relationship with Christ. What ultimately sealed the deal for him with Ole Miss had nothing to do with basketball and everything to do with the team chaplain and the local chapter of Fellowship of Christian Athletes.

For Todd Abernethy, life at Ole Miss wasn't so much about playing basketball as it was about glorifying Christ.

Most worthwhile aspects of life take time and tending to grow from small beginnings into something magnificent. A good marriage is that way. Your beautiful lawn just didn't appear. Old friends get that way after years of cultivation. And children don't get to be responsible and caring adults overnight.

Your faith, too, must be nurtured over time. Remember those older folks you revered as saints when you were growing up? Such distinction is achieved, not awarded. That is, they didn't start out that way. They were mature Christians because they walked and talked with Jesus; they prayed; they studied God's word; they helped others. They nourished and tended their faith with constant, loving care and attention.

In your faith as in other areas of your life, it's OK to start small. Faith is a journey, not a destination. You keep growing as those saints did, always moving on to bigger and better things in God.

I met a lot of strong Christian people down here, and I realized that Ole Miss would be the place I could grow the most spiritually.
-- Todd Abernethy on why he chose to play for Ole Miss

Faith is a lifelong journey of growth.

TOP SECRET

Read Romans 2:1-16.

"This will take place on the day when God will judge men's secrets through Jesus Christ, as my gospel declares" *(v. 16).*

The 1946 football season at Ole Miss was a bleak one with a head coach who would stay for that year only. The long season had a secret, though, that would change the fortunes of Rebel football.

Despite the success of a 31-8-1 record his first four seasons, head coach Harry Mehre couldn't recover from the damage wreaked by World War II. Only the urging of team captain Bob McCain, quarterback Johnny Bruce, and some other players kept alumni leaders from firing Mehre two games into the 1945 season. He was let go at season's end after a fourth straight losing campaign.

The new boss man was Harold Drew, long an ends coach at Alabama. As one writer described the '46 season, though, "Drew took command of a limping ship, and he never got it to port."

Drew's first game was an embarrassment for the program when the season opener against Kentucky arrived and Ole Miss didn't have any uniforms to play in. Drew borrowed some discards from Alabama, but most of the uniforms didn't fit. "Some of the pants Alabama sent to Lexington were so small they resembled shorts."

The season included another embarrassment, a loss to then-tiny Louisiana Tech at home. The final record was 2-7, and Drew left in January 1947 to take the head job at Alabama.

On the coaching staff that long season, however, was a secret, a relatively unknown line coach who had come to Ole Miss after serving in the Navy during World War II. The word soon circulated around town "that the big Texan was the backbone of the staff." As one player put it, "If we had anything at halftime in 1946, [the line coach] showed us. He could go to the blackboard and help you. The others just jumped up and down and cussed."

That not-so-well-kept secret was Johnny Vaught.

We have to be vigilant about the personal information that we prefer to keep secret. Much information about us -- from credit reports to what movies we rent -- is readily available to prying and persistent persons. In our information age, people we don't know may know a lot about us — or at least they can find out. And some of them may use this information for harm.

While diligence may allow us to be reasonably successful in keeping some secrets from the world at large, we should never deceive ourselves into believing we are keeping secrets from God. God knows everything about us, including the things we wouldn't want proclaimed at church. All our sins, mistakes, failures, shortcomings, quirks, prejudices, and desires – God knows all our would-be secrets.

But here's something God hasn't kept a secret: No matter what he knows about us, he loves us still.

The secret to winning is constant, consistent management.
-- Tom Landry

We have no secrets before God,
and it's no secret that he nevertheless loves us still.

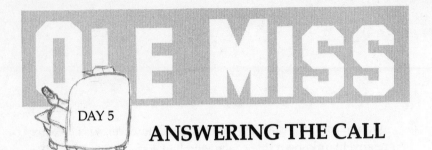

ANSWERING THE CALL

Read 1 Samuel 3:1-18.

"The Lord came and stood there, calling as at the other times, 'Samuel! Samuel!' Then Samuel said, 'Speak, for your servant is listening'" (v. 10).

They answered the call -- one Rebel backup after another. In part because of their courage and pluck, Ole Miss had a huge win over Auburn.

The 20th-ranked Rebs were 7-2 and in the hunt for the SEC West title when they went to Auburn on Nov. 7, 2003. As the physical game wore on, though, they were also beaten up. Three offensive linemen went down, and "the sideline was like a small infirmary for great big people." The situation was so bad that Stacy Andrews, who had never played organized football before the 2003 season, was in at right tackle.

He was just one, though, of "a cast of second- and third-team players forced into action at critical stages." The most critical of all came with under seven minutes to play with the Rebels trailing 20-17 and sitting at their own 19. Andrews was in, but he wasn't alone. Bobby Harris and Chris Spencer were with him in the patched-up offensive line. Before they all trotted onto the field, senior quarterback Eli Manning had been with them on the sideline trying to "make sure [they] understood our two-minute offense and what they needed to do."

They did.

REBELS

The Rebels went 81 yards in nine plays with Manning hitting all three of this passes. One of the key plays was a flat pass on third-and-five to fullback Lorenzo Townsend, who turned it into a 48-yard play to the Auburn 12. He had begun the season as the team's third-team fullback. It was the longest play of his career.

That set up the game winner, a one-yard plunge from Brandon Jacobs, the backup tailback. Jacobs went in behind guard Marcus Johnson and two guys named Spencer and Andrews. Right to the finish, all those backups answered the call.

Ole Miss won 24-20.

A team player is someone who does whatever the coach calls upon him to do for the good of the team. Something quite similar occurs when God places a specific call upon a Christian's life.

This is much scarier, though, than being called on by football coaches to play in a game. The way many folks understand it is that answering God's call means going into the ministry, packing the family up, and moving halfway around the world to some place where folks have never heard of air conditioning, fried chicken, or the Rebels. Zambia. The Philippines. Cleveland even.

Not for you, no thank you. And who can blame you?

But God usually calls folks to serve him where they are. In fact, God put you where you are right now, and he has a purpose in placing you there. Wherever you are, you are called to serve him.

Our guys found a way.
-- Defensive coordinator Chuck Driesbach on the Auburn win

**God calls you to serve him right now
right where he has put you, wherever that is.**

GOOD ADVICE

Read Isaiah 8:11-9:7.

"And he will be called Wonderful Counselor" (v. 9:6b).

The father found his son on his bed crying and asked him what was wrong. "I don't know if I can make it," was the reply. The son then got a little fatherly advice that forever changed Ole Miss football history.

The talented youngster torn by doubt and anxiety that December night in 1966 was Archie Manning. In retrospect, of course, this self-doubt by a boy who would become a legend may well strike us as laughable. But young Archie Manning could plainly see the obstacles that faced him. Signing with Ole Miss meant he would be one of eight quarterbacks the Rebels would bring to Oxford that year, several of them from the state's prestigious and powerful Big Eight Conference. "I'm 160 pounds from Drew, where we'd won five games my senior year, which was four more than we had won the year before," Manning recalled.

He had always wanted to go to Ole Miss. "But when it came time to make a decision, I couldn't," he remembered. He just wasn't sure he could make it. Thus came the tears that fateful night, along with Buddy Manning's timely appearance and even more timely advice, for which Rebel fans the world over will be forever grateful.

The father advised his son not to worry about how many other quarterbacks would be on hand or how impressive their credentials were. "They wouldn't want you at Ole Miss if they didn't think you can play," said dad to son. . . . "If you have made up your mind that's where you want to go, you shouldn't change it."

And so he didn't.

Like a young Archie Manning, we all need a little advice now and then. More often that not, we turn to professional counselors, who are all over the place. Marriage counselors, grief counselors, guidance counselors in our schools, rehabilitation counselors, all sorts of mental health and addiction counselors -- we even have pet counselors. No matter what our situation or problem, we can find plenty of advice for the taking.

The problem, of course, is that we find advice easy to offer but hard to swallow. We also have a rueful tendency to solicit the wrong source for advice, seeking counsel that doesn't really solve our problem but that instead enables us to continue with it.

Our need for outside advice, for an independent perspective on our situation, is actually God-given. God serves many functions in our lives, but one role clearly delineated in his Word is that of Counselor. Jesus himself is described as the "Wonderful Counselor." All the advice we need in our lives is right there for the asking; we don't even have to pay for it except with our faith. God is always there for us: to listen, to lead, and to guide.

All I needed was for [my dad] to say something. That made up my mind.
-- Archie Manning on his father's advice

We all need and seek advice in our lives,
but the ultimate and most wonderful Counselor
is of divine and not human origin.

DAY 7

ULTIMATE MAKEOVER

Read 2 Corinthians 5:11-21.

"If anyone is in Christ, he is a new creation; the old has gone, the new has come!" (v. 17)

Lauren Grill is, no doubt, the best of her sport ever to wear red and blue." Even so, the greatest softball player in Ole Miss history had to make herself over before her senior season.

From 2007-2010, Grill "pushed her program as far as anyone before her has." She was the first Ole Miss softball player in history to be named first team All-America and the first Rebel to be named All-SEC three times. She set school career records for hits, runs, RBIs, walks, total bases, batting average, on-base percentage, and slugging percentage. As one writer put it, "pretty much everything."

But as she prepared for her senior season, Grill decided she needed to make a major change in her approach to hitting. As a sophomore, she hit .393, but her production dropped her junior season. Her home runs fell from twelve to ten and she had a career-low .301 batting average. She knew why.

In her desire to help her team, she had spent the season hacking at pitches outside the strike zone instead of taking the walks opposing pitchers were more than willing to give her. "I've kind of learned," she said before her senior season, "that people are going to be careful when they're throwing to me. . . . People are going to throw a lot of pitches outside and a lot of changeups."

So Grill didn't need to get stronger or faster or improve her hand-eye coordination. She just had to make herself over into a patient hitter, which wasn't her natural approach at the plate.

That discipline put her right back into All-American form. In 2010, she led the team with a .444 batting average and also led the squad in home runs, RBIs, and slugging percentage. Her new-found patience at the plate led to a remarkable .571 on-base percentage, the fourth-best mark in SEC history.

Ever considered a makeover? TV shows show us how changes in clothes, hair, and makeup and some weight loss can radically alter the way a person looks. But these changes are only skin deep. Even with a makeover, the real you — the person inside — remains unchanged. How can you make over that part of you?

By giving your heart and soul to Jesus -- just as you give up your hair to the makeover stylist. You won't look any different; you won't dance any better; you won't suddenly start talking smarter. The change is on the inside where you are brand new because the model for all you think and feel is now Jesus. He is the one you care about pleasing. Made over by Jesus, you realize that gaining his good opinion — not the world's — is all that really matters. And he isn't the least interested in how you look but how you act.

If they're not going to throw to me, I'm still getting on base. That's the ultimate goal. That's what you need to win.
                                        -- Lauren Grill on her approach to hitting in 2010

Jesus is the ultimate makeover artist; he can make you over without changing the way you look.

MEMORY LOSS

Read 1 Corinthians 11:17-29.

"[D]o this in remembrance of me" (v. 24).

The two men watched it all and then committed it to memory "so we would never forget."

The duo was Ole Miss head coach David Cutcliffe and junior running back Deuce McAllister. What they watched so grimly was Mississippi State fans gleefully storming Scott Field in celebration of their team's win in the 1999 Egg Bowl. The pair wanted to remember the scene so the memory would drive them to make sure they didn't see it again in 2000. They didn't.

In 2000 the Rebels erased those haunting memories of '99 forever. They scored seventeen unanswered points over the last 22 minutes of the game to whip State 45-30.

The game was played amid attempts to make the experience more civil. The bands jointly played the national anthem before the game. School officials reinstated the original, more dignified postgame presentation of the Golden Egg that involved the presidents of both universities and the governor. As expected, however, the game itself was still the same old-fashioned slugfest.

State jumped out to an early 16-0 lead, conjuring up unpleasant memories for Cutcliffe, McAllister, and the legends of Ole Miss fans who remembered the season before. But the Rebs rallied with quarterback Romaro Miller hitting Grant Heard for a touchdown and then scrambling for fifty yards to the State 1. McAllister finished it from there, and when Miller found Heard for another score, Ole Miss led 21-16.

Apparently remembering their comeback the year before, the Bulldogs in turn rallied to lead 30-28. After that, though, Ole Miss scored 17 points to pull away. McAllister certainly did his part to erase the bad memories from the season before with 121 yards, three rushing touchdowns, and a tricky TD pass to Miller.

Memory makes us who we are. Whether our memories are dreams or nightmares, they shape us and to a large extent determine both our actions and our reactions. Alzheimer's is so terrifying because it steals our memory from us, and in the process we lose ourselves. We disappear.

The greatest tragedy of our lives is that God remembers. In response to that memory, he condemns us for our sin. On the other hand, the greatest joy of our lives is that God remembers. In response to that memory, he came as Jesus to wash even the memory of our sins away.

Through memory, we encounter revival. At the Last Supper, Jesus instructed his disciples and us to remember. In sharing this unique meal with fellow believers and remembering Jesus and his actions, we meet Christ again, not just as a memory but as an actual living presence. To remember is to keep our faith alive.

I don't want them to forget Babe Ruth. I just want them to remember Hank Aaron.

-- Hank Aaron

**We remember Jesus,
and God will not remember our sins.**

DAY 9

A SECOND CHANCE

Read John 7:53-8:11.

*"'Then neither do I condemn you,' Jesus declared. 'Go
now and leave your life of sin'" (v. 8:11).*

The Rebs once got a second chance they didn't want or need,
and the result was a wild controversy.

Only a 6-6 deadlock with LSU kept the Rebels of 1960 from an
undefeated, untied season, but it didn't keep them from a second
national championship. They pretty much coasted through the
regular season -- except for the Arkansas game. On Oct. 22 in
Little Rock, the two teams battled in what quarterback Jake Gibbs
called "one of the most physical games I ever played in."

With the score tied at seven and time running out, senior Allen
Green drilled a 39-yard field goal, and Rebel fans began celebrating. But wait! The referee had whistled the play dead just before
the snap because of the crowd noise. He said he halted the action
"because two or three players said they could not hear the signals.
The crowd was too loud."

So the teams rehuddled and the Rebels got ready for a second
chance at the game-winning kick. Gibbs told Green, "Keep your
head down. Don't worry about anything else."

The ref whistled the start of the play with only three seconds
left. Gibbs took the snap, set the ball down, and Green kept his
head down. The ball started out perfectly -- and then hooked as
it neared the goalposts.

REBELS

The official who had stopped play signaled the kick was good. The entire state of Arkansas thought otherwise. Certainly the ball landed outside the left post. Some Arkansas players said they went to the dressing room thinking they had won the game.

The Rebels knew otherwise. "The second one went through all right," said Green. Gibbs agreed, saying it barely cleared the goalposts. The ref simply said, "If it hadn't been good, I wouldn't have called it good."

"If I just had a second chance, I know I could make it work out." Ever said that? If only you could go back and tell your dad one last time you love him, take that job you passed up rather than relocate, or replace those angry shouts at your son with gentle encouragement. If only you had a second chance, a mulligan.

As the story of Jesus' encounter with the adulterous woman illustrates, with God you always get a second chance. No matter how many mistakes you make, God will never give up on you. Nothing you can do puts you beyond God's saving power. You always have a second chance because with God your future is not determined by your past or who you used to be. It is determined by your relationship with God through Jesus Christ.

God is ready and willing to give you a second chance – or a third chance or a fourth chance – if you will give him a chance.

I have to thank God for giving me the gift that he did as well as a second chance for a better life.
-- Olympic figure skating champion Oksana Baiul

**You get a second chance with God
if you give him a chance.**

HOW WE LEAVE

Read 2 Kings 2:1-12.

*"A chariot of fire and horses of fire appeared and separated
the two of them, and Elijah went up to heaven in a
whirlwind" (v. 11).*

Ole Miss once fired a coach who was so graceful about it that he
sent two sons back to Oxford to play for the Rebs.

"I always felt he was mistreated in 1929." So declared Claude
"Tadpole" Smith (See Devotion No. 64.) about Rebel head football
coach Homer Hazel. Hazel came to Oxford in 1925 with credentials as a two-time All-America at Rutgers.

The new head coach arrived at a time when the Ole Miss football program was in pretty bad shape. After four straight losing
seasons and -- most galling of all -- twelve straight losses to Mississippi A&M (State), the alums had had enough. The president of
the alumni association publicly declared that it was time for the
university to "start beating A&M in all departments of athletics."
The association went out, found, and hired Hazel.

The impact of this new coach with a relentless work ethic was
immediate. The Rebels of '25 went 5-5, the best record in eleven
years. After a 6-0 loss to A&M to end the season, Hazel vowed
that Ole Miss would never again lose to A&M on his watch. He
made good on his promise.

Three straight winning seasons followed, but in 1929 the Rebs
fell to 1-6-2. The decision was made to fire the coach. "Hazel was

a hero," to his players, said Smith, one of those players. "He was a great disciplinarian and I loved him."

Smith left with a 3-1-1 record against State and 21 career wins, at that time the most in school history. He "took his firing philosophically" and "never regretted his days in Oxford," even though he had turned down the head job at North Dakota before the 1929 season. Hazel was so graceful about what must have been painful for him that he eventually sent two sons -- Bill and Homer, Jr. -- down South from Michigan to play for the Rebels.

Like Homer Hazel and Elijah, we can't always choose the exact circumstances under which we leave. You probably haven't always chosen the moves you've made in your life. Perhaps your company transferred you. An elderly parent needed your care. Sometimes the only choice we have about leaving is the manner in which we go, whether we depart with style and grace or not.

Our exit from life is the same way. Unless we usurp God's authority over life and death, we can't choose how we die, just how we handle it. Perhaps the most frustrating aspect of dying is that we have at most very little control over the process. As with our birth, our death is in God's hands. We finally must surrender to his will even if we have spent a lifetime refusing to do so.

We do, however, control our destination. How we leave isn't up to us; where we spend eternity is -- and that depends on our relationship with Jesus.

If I drop dead tomorrow, at least I know I died in good health.
-- Former pro football coach Bum Phillips after a physical

How you go isn't up to you; where you go is.

YOUNG BLOOD

Read Jeremiah 1:4-10.

"The Lord said to me, 'Do not say, 'I am only a child' . . .
for I am with you and will rescue you" (vv. 7a, 8).

Vivian Vlaar didn't know what to expect when she arrived in Oxford. She certainly didn't expect to be the baby on the Ole Miss tennis team -- or on the whole campus for that matter.

Rebel tennis coach Mark Beyers discovered Vlaar in her native Belgium while he was recruiting her older sister. When his recruit decided to attend LSU, Beyers turned his attention to the younger sibling. Vivian had begun playing tennis when she was 3, and when she was 13, she began traveling and playing tournaments around the world.

Beyers had no doubts about Vlaar's ability, but he did have a concern: She was so young. Vlaar finished high school two years early in Belgium. Thus, when she arrived in Oxford in August of 2010 -- the first time she had ever even visited the United States -- she was only 16 years old. "There is a big difference between someone who is 16 and someone who is 20," Beyers noted.

Much about her new home was new and unexpected for the teenager, but she was especially surprised to find herself the youngest person around. "I didn't really know that everyone was at least 18 and would be older than me," she said.

Her age turned out to be a bigger deal for her fellow students than it was for Vlaar, who wound up getting quite irritated by a constant barrage of questions about her tender years. Her teammates, however, accepted her without question, no matter how young she was. "She's doing great for her age," said senior Laura van de Stroet. "I don't think I could have done any better."

Vlaar certainly matured quickly on the courts. The 16- and 17-year-old freshman played at No. 5 and No. 6 in the Rebels' singles lineup for 2010-11. She finished the fall and spring seasons with a 25-9 record, tying senior Connor Vogel for most wins.

While the media seem inordinately obsessed with youth, most aspects of our society value experience and some hard-won battle scars. Life usually requires us to spend time on the bench as a reserve, waiting for our chance to play with the big boys and girls. You probably rode some pine in high school. You started college as a lowly freshman. You began work at an entry-level position. Even head football coaches learn their trade as assistants.

Paying your dues is traditional, but that should never stop you from doing something bold right away, as Vivian Vlaar did her freshman year. Nowhere is this truer than in your faith life.

You may well assert that you are too young and too inexperienced to really do anything for God. Those are just excuses, however, and God won't pay a lick of attention to them when he issues a call. After all, the younger you are, the more time you have to serve.

When I think that I'll graduate at the age of 20, it's kind of creepy.
-- Vivian Vlaar on starting Ole Miss when she was 16

Youth is no excuse for not serving God;
it just gives you more time.

REVELATION

Read Isaiah 53.

"But he was pierced for our transgressions, he was crushed for our iniquities; the punishment that brought us peace was upon him, and by his wounds we are healed" (v. 5).

We're going to win them all." And thus did Ole Miss' junior halfback/defensive back Billy Kinard turn out to be a prophet.

Kinard spoke his words of prophecy at a most unlikely time. The Rebels had won the SEC in 1954 behind a defense that finished No. 1 in the nation by allowing only 172.3 yards per game. Tackle Rex Boggan was All-America. The consensus was that the road to the SEC title would pass through Oxford again in '55.

That prediction appeared quite farfetched, however, when Kentucky nailed the Rebels 21-14 in the second game of the season. About two hundred disappointed but faithful fans met the team bus when it pulled onto the campus, and right then and there, Kinard uttered his prophecy. As he walked through the crowd, he raised a fist, and declared, "We're going to win them all."

His prediction -- or declaration of defiance and hope -- was right on. The Rebels won eight straight games to finish the season at 9-1. They became only the third team in SEC history to capture back-to-back championships.

In the Rebels' 26-0 thrashing of State in the Egg Bowl, junior fullback and kicker Paige Cothren scored five points with his toe to win the SEC scoring title. Having been called "the best blocking fullback I have seen in years" by Georgia head coach Wally Butts, Cothren won the Jacobs Trophy as the league's best blocker.

The Rebs then slipped past TCU 14-13 in the Cotton Bowl to gain their first-ever win in a major bowl and to finish off exactly what Kinard had predicted: They won them all.

In our jaded age, we have pretty much relegated prophecy to dark rooms in which mysterious women peer into crystal balls or clasp our sweaty palms while uttering some vague generalities. At best, we understand a prophet as someone who predicts future events as Billy Kinard did in 1955.

Within the pages of the Bible, though, we encounter something radically different. A prophet is a messenger from God, one who relays divine revelation to others.

Prophets seem somewhat foreign to us because in one very real sense the age of prophecy is over. In the name of Jesus, we have access to God through our prayers and through scripture. In searching for God's will for our lives, we seek divine revelation. We may speak only for ourselves and not for the greater body of Christ, but we do not need a prophet to discern what God would have us do. We need faith in the one whose birth, life, and death fulfilled more than three hundred Bible prophecies.

I gave up a long time ago trying to predict the future and trying to deal with things I couldn't deal with.

-- *Brett Favre*

**Persons of faith continuously seek
a word from God for their lives.**

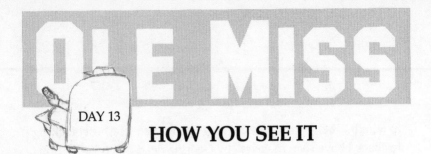

HOW YOU SEE IT

Read John 20:11-18.

"Mary stood outside the tomb crying" (v. 11).

Whether the Rebels had pulled out one of the most exciting and biggest upsets in Egg Bowl history or the Bulldogs had had the game stolen from them depended upon your point of view.

The 1981 Egg Bowl was a mismatch on paper. State was ranked No. 7 in the nation while the Rebels came in with six losses. But senior quarterback John Fourcade led a valiant Rebel effort that battled the Bulldogs to a 14-14 tie as the fourth quarter ticked away. His 10-yard TD run and the extra point with 3:37 to play tied the game. Then came what was called "the wildest ending ever" in the series.

The Bulldogs rushed back down the field and booted a field goal with 35 seconds left for a 17-14 lead. "Thousands headed for the exits, thinking that the game was over." They missed perhaps the most controversial ending in Egg Bowl history.

After State's kickoff was short and returned by Danny Jansen to the Rebel 40, Fourcade had 26 seconds to work with. He found his favorite receiver, split end Michael Harmon, for 19 yards and then for 16 more to the State 25. The clock showed thirteen seconds.

Fourcade went for Harmon again, but the State defender apparently hauled down an interception at the goal line. There was a whole lot of pushing and shoving on the play, and "as the Bulldogs screamed in protest and the Rebels cheered," a yellow flag fluttered gently to the ground. Pass interference. The Rebels got the ball at the State 1. On the next play, Fourcade swept around his right end for the game-winning touchdown. The clock had two ticks left.

The State defender told the papers he thought he was the one who was interfered with. Harmon countered that the interference call was the right one, that the defender "bumped me and kind of pushed me." It was all a matter of perspective -- expect for the final 21-17 score.

Your perspective goes a long way toward determining whether you slink through life amid despair, anger, and hopelessness or stride boldly through life with joy and hope. Mary Magdalene is an excellent example. On that first Easter morning, she stood by Jesus' tomb crying, her heart broken, because she still viewed everything through the perspective of Jesus' death. But how her attitude, her heart, and her life changed when she saw the morning through the perspective of Jesus' resurrection.

So it is with life and death for all of us. You can't avoid death, but you can determine how you perceive it. Is it fearful, dark, fraught with peril and uncertainty? Or is it a simple little passageway to glory, the light, and loved ones, an elevator ride to paradise?

It's a matter of perspective that depends totally on whether or not you're standing by Jesus' side when it arrives.

The official made the call, and that's that.
— State head coach Emory Bellard's perspective on the interference call

**Whether death is your worst enemy
or a solicitous chauffeur is a matter of perspective.**

GOOD-BYE

Read John 13:33-38.

"My children, I will be with you only a little longer" (v. 33a).

The Rebels had such a good time saying good-bye they didn't want to leave.

In 1936, a Dallas oilman watched the Rose Bowl and figured his hometown should have a New Year's Day game too. The next year, the Cotton Bowl was born, played in the stadium of the same name. On Jan. 1, 2009, the Cotton Bowl was played in the stadium for the 73rd and final time, and the Rebels were there to help say good-bye to the storied old facility.

First-year Rebel head coach Houston Nutt grew up in Arkansas with the Cotton Bowl. "Mom had black-eyed peas going, and cornbread, and all of that, while we were getting ready to watch the Cotton Bowl," he remembered. And now his 20th-ranked and 8-4 Rebels were in the farewell game against the 8th-ranked and 11-1 Red Raiders of Texas Tech.

Quarterback Jevan Snead, tailback Dexter McCluster, and cornerback and punt returner Marshay Green led Ole Miss to a 47-34 smashing of the vaunted Raiders. Tech led early 14-0, but Snead led Ole Miss to touchdowns on its next three drives. A field goal after that put the Rebs in the lead for good. When Green returned an interception 65 yards for a touchdown in the third quarter, the Raiders never could catch up.

REBELS

The Rebels rolled up 515 yards of offense behind Snead's 292 yards and three touchdowns passing. Tight end Gerald Harris had only two catches, but both went for touchdowns. McCluster ran for 97 yards and a touchdown and caught six passes for 83 yards.

When the game was over, the Rebel players were reluctant to say good-bye. They did backflips at midfield, made a sprint to the student section, and dashed around carrying oversized flags.

You've stood on the curb and watched someone you love drive off, or you've grabbed a last-minute hug before a plane leaves. Maybe it was a child leaving home for the first time or your best friends moving halfway across the country. It's an extended – maybe even permanent – separation, and good-byes hurt.

Jesus felt the pain of parting too. Throughout his brief ministry, Jesus had been surrounded by and had depended upon his friends and confidants, the disciples. About to leave them, he gathered them for a going-away supper and gave them a heads-up about what was about to happen. In the process, he offered them words of comfort. What a wonderful friend he was! Even though he was the one who was about to suffer unimaginable agony, Jesus' concern was for the pain his friends would feel.

But Jesus wasn't just saying good-bye. He was on his mission of providing the way through which none of us would ever have to say good-bye again.

We'll make the announcement we'll come back next year, right now.
– Houston Nutt, not wanting to leave the Cotton Bowl

Through Jesus, we will see the day
when we say good-bye to good-byes.

WHAT YOU HAVE TO

Read 2 Samuel 12:1-15a.

"The Lord sent Nathan to David" (v. 1).

We did what we had to do to win," declared Ole Miss head basketball coach Bob Weltlich. That was in overtime, though. In the closing minutes of regulation, the Rebs seemed to be about the business of doing everything they could to lose.

The Rebels of 1980-81 would make school history by wining the SEC Tournament for the first time ever. On Jan. 24, though, such a lofty achievement was not on their minds as they struggled to keep a win over Mississippi State from slipping away.

Ole Miss seemed to have the game salted away with a 10-point lead and only 3:24 on the clock. But State started fouling intentionally, and the Rebels started missing free throws unintentionally. Four straight times in the last three minutes, a Rebel went to the line for a one-and-one and missed the first one. With a minute to go, State tied the game at 42.

Sensing a good thing, the Bulldogs fouled Chris Barrett with 55 seconds left. He ended the bleeding, though, by hitting a pair. State tied it with 45 ticks on the clock, and the Rebs called time out with 17 seconds left. One more time they didn't do what they had to do to claim the win: They never got off a shot. Overtime.

From then on, though, Weltlich was right; the Rebels did what they had to do. Right off the bat in the extra period, they got a breakaway layup from Cecil Dowell. After State tied the game with 3:35 left, the Rebs held the ball for almost two minutes before Carlos Clark broke loose for a layup. Then with 45 seconds left and the Rebs leading only 50-49, they again did what they had to. Sean Tuohy spotted Elston Turner loose under the basket and whipped a strike to him for a layup.

After all the team's miscues at the charity stripe in regulation, Tuohy hit six straight free throws in overtime.

Ole Miss finally did what it had to and won 59-52.

You've also had to do some things in your life that you really didn't want to do. Maybe when you put your daughter on severe restriction, broke the news of a death in the family, fired a friend, or underwent surgery. You plowed ahead because you knew it was for the best or you had no choice.

Nathan surely didn't want to confront King David and tell him what a miserable reprobate he'd been, but the prophet had no choice: Obedience to God overrode all other factors. Of all that God asks of us in the living of a godly life, obedience is perhaps the most difficult. After all, our history of disobedience stretches all the way back to the Garden of Eden.

The problem is that God expects obedience not only when his wishes match our own, but also when they don't. Obedience to God is a way of life, not a matter of convenience.

Coaching is making men do what they don't want, so they can become what they want to be.

-- Legendary NFL Coach Tom Landry

You can never foresee what God will demand of you, but obedience requires being ready to do whatever God asks.

THE LEADER

Read Matthew 16:18-23.

"You are Peter, and on this rock I will build my church, and the gates of Hades will not overcome it" (v. 18).

During the hot days of spring practice in preparation for the 2011 football season, the Rebels found their leader in a player many folks thought wouldn't even make a major-college team.

The experts decided Brandon Bolden was just an average high school recruit. Some SEC schools took a quick peek and backed away. LSU, twenty minutes away from Bolden's home town, never offered. Alabama and Ole Miss stayed in the hunt, and when new head coach Houston Nutt pursued Bolden, he committed.

And found himself way back in a whole pack of talented running backs at Oxford. From the first time he stepped onto an Ole Miss practice field, though, Bolden stood out. He was "far and away" more intense than anyone else on the roster. When the 2008 season began with a 41-24 win over Memphis, the freshman was the Rebels' leading rusher with 76 yards and a touchdown. He has been leading ever since, to the point that as the 2011 season neared, he was within sight of Deuce McAllister's school records for career rushing yards and touchdowns.

In the spring of 2011, first-year offensive coordinator David Lee decided to make Bolden's leadership official. He approached the rising senior, aware that he had led the 2010 team in rushing and receiving. At the time, Bolden was nursing an ankle injury as spring practice wound down.

"I'm new here and I don't know what's happened in the past," Lee told Bolden. Then he asked him point blank, "Are you ready to take a leadership role on this offensive football team this summer?" Bolden's reply was just as direct: "Yes, sir, I am."

Every aspect of life that involves people – every organization, every group, every project, every team -- must have a leader. If goals are to be reached, somebody must take charge.

Even the early Christian church was no different. Jesus knew this, so he designated the leader in Simon Peter, who was such an unlikely choice to assume such an awesome, world-changing responsibility that Jesus soon after rebuked him as "Satan."

In *Twelve Ordinary Men*, John MacArthur described Simon as "ambivalent, vacillating, impulsive, unsubmissive." Hardly a man to inspire confidence in his leadership skills. Yet, according to MacArthur, Peter became "the greatest preacher among the apostles" and the "dominant figure" in the birth of the church.

The implication for your own life is both obvious and unsettling. You may think you lack the attributes necessary to make a good leader for Christ. But consider Simon Peter, an ordinary man who allowed Christ to rule his life and became the foundation upon which the Christian church was built.

Anybody can go out there and shout and yell at guys to get their attention. I try to keep it quiet and lead by example.
-- Brandon Bolden

God's leaders are men and women
who allow Jesus to lead them.

OF GOOD CHEER

Read Matthew 21:1-11.

*"The crowds that went ahead of him and those that
followed shouted" (v. 9).*

The cheer that was the favorite among the Ole Miss student
body in 1910 isn't likely to make a return anytime soon, but they
sure had a lot to cheer about.

In 1909, university chancellor Andrew A. Kincannon made a
monumental decision that forever affected football at the school.
He hired the first-ever athletic director, taking athletics out of the
students' hands for the first time. For the job, he hired Dr. Nathan
P. Stauffer, who was an assistant football coach at Penn.

Stauffer stayed three seasons, compiling a 17-7-2 record and
forging the Rebels into a force in the Southern Intercollegiate Athletic Association. "The genial doctor brought bigtime football to
the University of Mississippi."

The highlight of Stauffer's brief time in Oxford was the 1910
season, the best in school history until the 1935 Orange Bowl
team. Led by right halfback John W. "Scotchy" McCall, the '10
team went 7-1, its only loss 9-2 to Vanderbilt, which was the only
team that even scored on the Rebs.

The highlight of the season was the season finale against Mississippi A&M (State). In a different age, A&M had asked Stauffer
to serve as an official in its game against Howard. A&M entered
the game in Jackson as the favorite, but the Ole Miss Red and Blue

REBELS

shocked five thousand interested observers with a 30-0 romp.

The season also included wins over Tulane and Alabama, so raucous cheers and the pealing of the Lyceum's bell were regular and rowdy sounds in 1910. And the cheer that was the students' personal favorite? "Boomalacka, Boomalacka, wow, wow, wow; Chickalack, Chickalack, chow, chow, chow; Boomalack, Chickalack, way, who, wah; Mississippi, Mississippi, rah rah rah!"

Chances are you go to work every day, do your job well, and then go home to your family. This country couldn't run without you; you're indispensable to the nation's efficiency. Even so, nobody cheers for you, waves pompoms in your face, or hollers "Boomalacka, Boomalacka" at you. Your name probably will never elicit a standing ovation when a PA announcer calls it.

It's just as well, since public opinion is notoriously fickle. Consider what happened to Jesus. When he entered Jerusalem, he was the object of raucous cheering and an impromptu parade. The crowd's adulation reached such a frenzy they tore branches off trees and threw their clothes on the ground.

Five days later the crowd shouted again, only this time they screamed for Jesus' execution.

So don't worry too much about not having your personal set of cheering fans. Remember that you do have one personal cheerleader who will never stop pulling for you: God.

A cheerleader is a dreamer that never gives up.

– Source unknown

**Just like the sports stars,
you do have a personal cheerleader: God.**

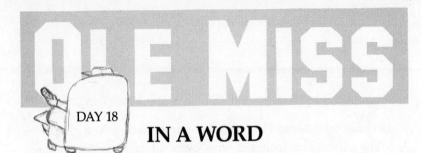

DAY 18

IN A WORD

Read Matthew 12:33-37.

"For out of the overflow of the heart the mouth speaks. The good man brings good things out of the good stored up in him, and the evil man brings evil things out of the evil stored up in him" (vv. 34b-35).

Though he was one of football's greatest quarterbacks, Charley Conerly preferred to speak through his actions, not his words.

"Taciturn Charles Albert Conerly, son of a railroad man, . . . never did a lot of talking." A sign in his office in later years said, "Speak softly and tenderly for tomorrow you may have to eat your words." He was a man who did much but said very little.

Friends and acquaintances had two explanations for Conerly's manner. Some said it was forged through the horrors he experienced as a Marine who participated in the invasion of Guam during World War II. Others asserted that because of his reputation as a young man who enjoyed raising a little Cain, with maturity came the decision to lead by example rather than words.

Asked once how he got the timing he used to throw a football, Conerly replied, "I've just kinda come to believe God gives everybody some talent. He gave it to me and I'd better use it the best way I can." He did.

He was All-SEC in 1946 though the Rebels were only 2-7. He was also the team's punter, averaging 42.8 yards a kick. In 1947, he was All-America as a senior under first-year coach Johnny Vaught, setting an NCAA record with 133 pass completions.

Conerly went on to become an All-Pro. He was the quarterback for the New York Giants in the 1958 NFL championship game that went into overtime and is often considered the greatest game ever played. He took the Giants to four championship games, winning it all in 1956.

And all the while, he didn't have much to say about it.

These days, everybody's got something to say and likely as not a place to say it. Talk radio, 24-hour sports and news TV channels, late-night talk shows. Talk has really become cheap.

But words still have power, and that includes not just those of the talking heads, hucksters, and pundits on television, but ours also. Our words are perhaps the most powerful force we possess for good or for bad. The words we speak today can belittle, wound, humiliate, and destroy. They can also inspire, heal, protect, and create. Our words both shape and define us. They also reveal to the world the depth of our faith.

We should never make the mistake of underestimating the power of the spoken word. After all, speaking the Word was the only means Jesus had to get his message across – and look what he managed to do.

We must always watch what we say, because others sure will.

[Charley Conerly's] quiet confidence commanded respect. He never yelled or berated anyone in the huddle.
-- Kyle Rote, a teammate of Conerly's in New York

Choose your words carefully; they are the most powerful force you have for good or for bad.

DAY 19

GREAT EXPECTATIONS

Read John 1:43-51.

"'Nazareth! Can anything good come from there?'
Nathanael asked" (v. 46).

Out of basketball for a year, Maggie McFerrin didn't really expect to walk on and make the Ole Miss team, let alone actually play. She should have raised her expectations a wee bit.

After a career at Tupelo High School that saw her make all-state in basketball, track and cross country, McFerrin pretty much gave up on competitive sports. Junior colleges and small schools were interested in her basketball skills, but she was drawn to Ole Miss. So in the fall of 2009, she came to Oxford and spent a year playing intramurals and scrimmaging with the guys. After all, Ole Miss coach Renee Ladner didn't hold walk-on tryouts.

But three interesting things happened. First, McFerrin got the itch again, especially when she held her own in pickup games against some of the varsity players. Secondly, Ladner found herself short of bodies and decided to hold try-outs. McFerrin didn't know it but she had an inside track. Those players who had scrimmaged with and against her sang the praises of "the girl from Tupelo" to Ladner. She made the team.

That was more than McFerrin expected. At her first practice, she said she was just happy to be there and didn't expect much playing time because she was "just a walk-on." The first time a coach signaled for her to report to the scorer's table, she thought,

"Oh my gosh, I'm about to go in."

She played some, and then a third thing happened: Senior Kayla Melson went down with a knee injury. On Feb. 6, 2011, the sophomore who never even expected to be on the team started against LSU. She went on to play in twenty games, starting six and averaging 16 minutes and 2.9 points per game.

The blind date your friend promised would look like Brad Pitt or Jennifer Aniston but resembled a Munster or Cousin Itt. Your vacation that went downhill after the lost luggage. Often your expectations are raised only to be dashed. Sometimes it's best not to get your hopes up; then at least you have the possibility of being surprised.

Worst of all, perhaps, is when you realize that you are the one not meeting others' expectations. The fact is, though, that you aren't here to live up to what others think of you. Jesus didn't; in part, that's why they killed him. But he did meet God's expectations for his life, which was all that really mattered.

Because God's kingdom is so great, God does have great expectations for any who would enter, and you should not take them lightly. What the world expects from you is of no importance; what God expects from you is paramount.

I just never thought . . . just making the team and playing, much less starting. I'm amazed.

-- Maggie McFerrin

You have little if anything to gain from meeting the world's expectations of you; you have all of eternity to gain from meeting God's.

DAY 20

DRY RUN

Read John 4:1-15.

"Everyone who drinks this water will be thirsty again,
but whoever drinks the water I give him will never thirst.
Indeed, the water I give him will become in him a spring
of water welling up to eternal life" (vv. 13-14).

No bowl trips in twelve seasons. No SEC win in almost two seasons. But the drought came to an end in one of the most exciting and dramatic games in Ole Miss football history.

The Vanderbilt Commodores were favored when the two teams met in Oxford on Oct. 22, 1983, and they took an early 7-0 lead. The Rebs tied it on a 1-yard run by tailback Buford McGee in the second quarter. They came from behind again to tie the game at 14 with only 52 seconds left in the half when Kelly Powell hit wide receiver Stephen Cunningham with a 14-yard toss. Ole Miss took the lead for the first time at 21-14 with exactly five minutes to go in the third quarter on a 37-yard, end-around run by Andre Rodgers. A third-down completion to Tim Moffett set up the score.

All that action served only as a preliminary for the finish that Ole Miss head coach Billy Brewer described as "slow death." The Commodores blocked a Rebel field-goal attempt that would have iced the game with 1:37 to play. They quickly moved to the Ole Miss 45, but the clock was down to 38 seconds.

Then, as the home crowd watched in horror, Vandy dropped a bomb to the tight end all the way to the Ole Miss 1. A quick pass

REBELS

out of bounds stopped the clock with 17 seconds left. Confusion led the Commodores to take an intentional delay-of-game penalty rather than waste a down, which moved the ball back to the 6.

Vanderbilt then threw into the end zone, and Rebel cornerback Eric Truitt made a dramatic, game-saving, and drought-ending interception. The clock showed only six seconds. The Rebs went on to whip LSU, Tennessee, and Mississippi State in succession, finish 6-5, and wind up in the Independence Bowl.

You can walk across that river you boated on in the spring. The city's put all neighborhoods on water restriction. That beautiful lawn you fertilized and seeded will turn a sickly, pale green and may lapse all the way to brown. Somebody wrote "Wash Me" on the rear window of your truck.

The sun bakes everything, including the concrete. The earth itself seems exhausted, just barely hanging on. It's a drought.

It's the way a soul that shuts God out looks.

God instilled thirst in us to warn us of our body's need for physical water. He also gave us a spiritual thirst that can be quenched only by his presence in our lives. Without God, we are like tumbleweeds, dried out and windblown, offering the illusion of life where there is only death.

Living water – water of life – is readily available in Jesus. We may drink our fill, and thus we slake our thirst and end our soul's drought – forever.

Drink before you are thirsty. Rest before you are tired.
-- Paul de Vivie, father of French cycle touring

Our soul thirsts for God's refreshing presence.

HUGS AND KISSES

Read John 15:5-17.

"Now remain in my love" (v. 9b).

It's not every day you see a head coach get hugged by players from both teams after a game. It happened, though, in 2008 to first-year Ole Miss head coach Houston Nutt.

The Rebels were 3-4 and not at all confident as they prepared to take on Arkansas. After all, they had lost four straight to the Razorbacks. There was one big difference this year, however: Nutt had been on the Arkansas sideline for each of those wins; this time he was standing with the Red and Blue.

After ten seasons as the head coach at Arkansas, Nutt took over the Rebels in 2008. On Oct. 25, he returned to Fayetteville, this time as the enemy. "This game was different. It was emotional and it was very hard," Nutt admitted.

The biggest difference was that the Rebels won. Jevan Snead threw touchdown passes to Mike Wallace and Shay Hodge, and Joshua Shene kicked three field goals, the last with 1:45 to play, as the Rebs edged the Hogs 23-21.

The fans booed Nutt from the start, which came as no surprise to him. "I've been booed when I was on that sideline," he said, pointing to Arkansas' side of the field. One fan threw an empty water bottle at him. Another was ejected for throwing a cup of ice Nutt's way. He was hit by a spray of water as he led his jubilant Ole Miss team into the locker room after the win.

The reaction was much different from his formers players, however. After the game, he exchanged hugs with many of the Hogs. "You recruited them; you've been in their living room," he said. "It was harder than I thought." Arkansas center Jonathan Luigs was among those who purposefully greeted his former coach. "It's common courtesy with a guy you spent a lot of time with the last four years," he explained.

That friend from college you haven't seen for a while. Your family, including that aunt with the body odor. We hug them all, whether in greeting, in good-bye, or simply as a spontaneous display of affection. The act of physically clutching someone tightly to us symbolizes how closely we hold them in our hearts.

So whether you are a profligate hugger or a more judicious dispenser of your hugs, a hug is an act of intimacy. Given that, the ultimate hugger is Almighty God, who, through Christ, continuously seeks to draw us closer to him in love. A good hug, though, takes two, so what God seeks from us is to hug him back.

We do that by keeping him close in our hearts, by witnessing for his Son through both words and deeds. To live our lives for Jesus is to engage in one long refreshing, and heartwarming hug with God.

It is hard not to love players that you recruited and coached. You are close to them.
-- Houston Nutt on greeting his former players after the Arkansas game

A daily walk with Christ means we are
so close to God that we are engaged
in one long, joyous hug with the divine.

SIZE MATTERS

Read Luke 19:1-10.

[Zacchaeus] wanted to see who Jesus was, but being a
short man he could not, because of the crowd. So he ran
ahead and climbed a sycamore-fig tree to see him (vv. 3-4).

"If I have to play boys that size, I might as well go back to Georgia." In relying on size as a gauge, Ole Miss' head football coach had just misjudged two prospects who would become Rebel gridiron greats.

After being let go at Georgia, Harry Mehre came to Oxford in 1938 and became the winningest coach in school history (up to that time) over the next eight seasons. He turned the moribund program around his first season with a 9-2 record.

In 1938, Ike Knox, who had lettered in 1907 and '08 and would be a charter member of the Ole Miss Athletics Hall of Fame, introduced Mehre to two prospects, "both only slightly larger than a minute." They each weighed in at a whopping 135 pounds, eliciting Mehre's disparaging comments.

The prospects were Junie Hovious and Billy Sam. Sam was a three-year letterman (1939-41) at right half who was inducted into the Mississippi Sports Hall of Fame in 1965.

Described as "stumpy" and "little," Hovious had bulked up to all of 150 pounds by the 1939 season when he began a three-year run as the team's rushing star. In the 28-14 upset in 1940 of Mehre's former team, Hovious ripped off a 96-yard punt return.

REBELS

He was All-SEC three times and served 29 years at Ole Miss as an assistant football coach. He was also the Rebel golf coach for 25 years and was inducted into the school's hall of fame in 1987. Decades later, Mehre said Hovious had "talent that at the least is defined as greatness."

Despite having to play Sam and Hovious as he had feared he would, Mehre didn't go back to Georgia. He played them because they were so good, no matter what their size.

Bigger is better! Such is one of the most powerful mantras of our time. We expand our football stadiums. We augment our body parts. Hey, make that a triple cheeseburger and a large order of fries! My company is bigger than your company. Even our church buildings must be bigger to be better. About the only exception to our all-consuming drive for bigness is our waistlines.

But size obviously didn't matter to Jesus. After all, salvation came to the house of an evil tax collector who was so short he had to climb a tree to catch a glimpse of Jesus. Zacchaeus indeed had a big bank account; he was a big man in town even if his own people scorned him. But none of that – including Zacchaeus' height – mattered; Zacchaeus received salvation because of his repentance, which revealed itself in a changed life.

The same is true for us today. What matters is the size of the heart devoted to our Lord.

It is not the size of a man but the size of his heart that matters.
-- *Evander Holyfield*

**Size matters to Jesus, but only the size
of the heart of the one who would follow Him.**

DAY 23

IMPOSSIBLE DREAM

Read Matthew 19:16-26.

*"Jesus looked at them and said, 'With man this is
impossible, but with God all things are possible'" (v. 26).*

An Ole Miss lineman made a play against LSU that a sportswriter described as "impossible."

The Rebels of 1963 won the program's sixth SEC championship.
They went 7-0-2, with ties against Memphis State in the opener
and Mississippi State in the finale. The defense was the best in the
country and didn't allow more than one touchdown in any game.
Even in the 12-7 loss to Alabama in the Sugar Bowl, the Tide won
on four field goals.

The highlight of the season was 37-3 romp over bitter rival LSU
in Baton Rouge. Whaley Hall blocked a punt, and Reed Davis
recovered a fumble to get the romp under way. Fullback Freddie
Roberts scored three touchdowns.

The highlight of the game, however, was a play pulled off
by sophomore guard Stan Hindman. The Rebels were well on
their way to a win with a 23-3 lead when they punted. The Tiger
return man got a block at his own 18 and then set sail up the
sideline with nothing but grass in front of him. A writer from the
Times-Picayune described what happened. "Hindman, Ole Miss'
230-pound sophomore guard, did the impossible, catching [the
return man] from behind and knocking him out of bounds at the
Rebel one. How fast that makes Hindman is anybody's guess but

until Saturday [the LSU runner] was considered the fastest thing this side of Cape Canaveral."

After Hindman's "impossible" play, LSU ran four plays and wound up at the five. Instead of having a big play that would have electrified the crowd and put them right back in the game, the Tigers had nothing but blasted hopes.

Stan Hindman made an impossible play because he believed he could and he didn't quit. His action that day in Louisiana can serve as an inspiration to all people of faith.

Let's face it. Any pragmatic person, no matter how deep his faith, has to admit that the world is just an impossible mess. The only hope for this dying, sin-infested place lies in our Lord's return to set everything right.

But we can't just give up and sit around praying for Jesus' return, as glorious a day as that will be. Our mission in this world is to change it for Jesus. We serve a Lord who calls us to step out in faith into seemingly impossible situations. We serve a Lord so audacious that he inspires us to believe that we are the instruments through which God does the impossible.

Changing the world may indeed seem impossible. Changing our corner of it, however, is not. It is, rather, a very possible, doable act of faith.

The difference between the impossible and the possible lies in a person's determination.

-- Tommy Lasorda

**With God, nothing is impossible,
including changing the world for Jesus.**

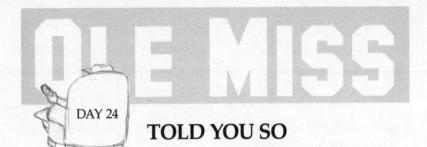

DAY 24

TOLD YOU SO

Read Matthew 24:15-31.

"See, I have told you ahead of time" (v. 25).

Before one of the biggest games in school basketball history, head coach Rob Evans told his players what they should say after they won. And so they did.

The Rebels of 1996-97 went 20-9, the program's first 20-win season since coach George Bohler's 22-12 squad of 1937-38. They were champions of the SEC's West Division and notched the program's second-ever trip to the NCAA Tournament.

The team was on a mission to prove itself, to garner respect for the program. When Evans took over before the 1993-94 season, the Rebels had had only two winning seasons in the previous thirteen. Arkansas head coach Nolan Richardson said that when his team played Ole Miss, it had about a 90 percent chance of winning. Then Richardson added, "Those chances have diminished greatly since Rob took over."

Despite their 10-3 record, the Rebs hadn't gained any national respect or recognition. They were looking for the program's first-ever ranking in the AP polls when they welcomed third-ranked Kentucky on Jan. 11. More than 8,000 fans filled up Tad Smith Coliseum to see if their team was for real. Evans sure thought so. He was so sure that before the game, he told his players exactly how they should go about saying "I told you so" after the game.

Solid, defense-minded athletes made up that squad; it was led

REBELS

by junior forwards Ansu Sesay and Anthony Boone, who came back from two knee surgeries to play.

They went out and whipped Kentucky 73-69. And what exactly had Evans said to his team before the game? "After you've won the game, I want you to tell the press this is not a fluke," he said. "You're for real." When junior guard Joezon Darby met the press, he said exactly that, telling the nation, "I told you so."

The Rebels cracked the Top 20 the next week.

Don't you just hate it in when somebody says, "I told you so"? That means the other person was right and you were wrong; that other person has spoken the truth. You could have listened to that know-it-all in the first place, but then you would have lost the chance yourself to crow, "I told you so."

In our pluralistic age and society, many view truth as relative, meaning absolute truth does not exist. All belief systems have equal value and merit. But this is a ghastly, dangerous fallacy because it ignores the truth that God proclaimed in the presence and words of Jesus.

In speaking the truth, Jesus told everybody exactly what he was going to do: come back and take his faithful followers with him. Those who don't listen or who don't believe will be left behind with those four awful words, "I told you so," ringing in their ears and wringing their souls.

We'll win this game. I guarantee it.
-- Joe Namath before the 1969 Super Bowl, which his Jets won

Jesus matter-of-factly told us what he has planned:
He will return to gather all the faithful to himself.

THE GAME OF LIFE

Read 1 Corinthians 9:24-27.

Run in such a way as to get the prize (v. 24b).

Too bad for Nebraska their meeting with the Rebels wasn't a video game. Instead, it was football.

As part of the festivities prior to the 2002 Independence Bowl, Nebraska and Mississippi players engaged in a cyber showdown. That is, they played a lot of video games against each other. The Cornhuskers blew the Rebels away, but as one writer declared, "Big-time football is played on the field, not in an arcade." And on the field -- where it mattered -- the Rebels pulled off a 27-23 upset, "jolt[ing] the Cornhuskers with a swift dose of reality."

Pre-game hype said the Rebel defense couldn't stop Big Red's vaunted running attack. The talking heads focused on Nebraska's power in the trenches and paid little attention to the speed the Reb defense would throw at the Cornhuskers.

In the end, the defense made all the difference. Nebraska did rush for 266 yards, but most of the damage was done between the 20-yard lines. Nobody scores points out there. The Huskers could score only one touchdown on the ground. By the fourth quarter, the Rebel defense had complete control of the game, holding Nebraska to four yards on twelve runs in the last quarter. "In the third quarter," said senior linebacker Eddie Strong, "I could start to tell that we were getting to them. They weren't as physical."

The defense, in fact, turned the game around with a play in

the first half. Nebraska led 10-0 and was dominating until Von Hutchins intercepted a pass and returned it to the Husker 27. Six plays later, Eli Manning hit Kerry Johnson over the middle for an 11-yard TD.

It was just the kind of killer play the Huskers had made in the video games, the ones that didn't matter.

Life may be a game, but where are the rules? Who sets them or does everybody play by his or her own rules? What is the object of the game? How do we win, since every life ends in the same way – with death – and there's really no set time when or specified manner how that end occurs? What's the prize for winning?

If life is a game, it's a chaotic one that really doesn't make any sense at all. Unless the game is played according to the rules set up the master gamer of them all, Almighty God. His rules are spelled out quite clearly in his instruction book. The game according to God has a clearly defined object: to glorify Him.

Most importantly, the life as played God's way has clearly defined winners and losers. The winners are those who seek out God and find their salvation in Jesus Christ. And the prize for winning is the greatest grand prize of them all: eternal life in Heaven.

Play ball.

Boxing is the ultimate game of life. When you get knocked down, you get back up.

-- Boxing coach Mike Johnson

**Life played God's way is the most exciting
and rewarding game of them all.**

DAY 26

AS A RULE

Read Luke 5:27-32.

"Why do you eat and drink with tax collectors and 'sinners'?" (v. 30b)

An Ole Miss football player once did something so shocking during a game that a rule was passed to make sure he didn't do it again.

Even in the 1920s, football's rules were somewhat loose. For instance, halfback Claude "Tadpole" Smith (See Devotion 64.) refused to wear a helmet because he believed it slowed him down. "The helmets in those days were made about like helmets worn by boxers in training," recalled tackle Thad "Pie" Vann, one of Smith's teammates who had a hall-of-fame career as the head coach at Southern Miss. To further reduce wind resistance, Smith taped his ears back, and Vann got Smith to show him how to do it. "I played several games without a helmet," Vann said.

In the second game of 1927, the Rebs took on Florida in Gainesville. Team captain Austin Applewhite scored on a pass from Harvey Walker that was the difference in the 12-7 Rebel win.

Applewhite generated quite a controversy in the game, but it wasn't because of the touchdown he scored. In response to the Florida heat, he took his jersey off. A somewhat surprised Gator head coach vehemently insisted that the rules said Applewhite had to wear a jersey. When a ref told the Rebel captain to put his jersey back on, Applewhite replied that if the official could show him in the rules book where a jersey was required, he would wear it. There was no such rule.

Thus, Applewhite scored his game-winning touchdown shirtless. After the season, the college rules committee met and added a rule that required the wearing of jerseys in a game.

You live by rules that others set up. Some lender determined the interest rate on your mortgage and your car loan. You work hours and shifts somebody else established. Someone else decided what day your garbage gets picked up and what school district your house is in.

Jesus encountered societal rules also, including a strict set of religious edicts that dictated what company he should keep, what people, in other words, were fit for him to socialize with, talk to, or share a meal with. Jesus ignored the rules, choosing love instead of mindless obedience and demonstrating his disdain for society's rules by mingling with the outcasts, the lowlifes, the poor, and the misfits.

You, too, have to choose when you find yourself in the presence of someone whom society deems undesirable. Will you choose the rules or love? Are you willing to be a rebel for love — as Jesus was for you?

I believe in rules. Sure I do. If there weren't any rules, how could you break them?

-- Baseball Hall of Famer Leo Durocher

**Society's rules dictate who is acceptable
and who is not, but love in the name of Jesus
knows no such distinctions.**

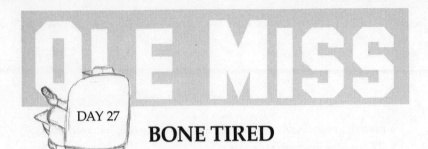

BONE TIRED

Read Matthew 11:27-30.

"Come to me, all you who are weary and burdened, and I will give you rest" (v. 11).

An exhausted Rebel running back once came up with a novel way to get a break during a game.

Johnny Vaught's 1948 team rolled to an 8-1 record, only a loss to Tulane costing them a second straight SEC title. The star of the team was three-time All-American end Barney Poole. Because he played for Army during World War II and service time didn't count against eligibility, Poole played seven seasons of college football. The quarterback of the '48 team was Farley Salmon, who stood only 5-8. (See Devotion No. 45.) He called Poole "a great team man" and lamented that "I couldn't see over the people to throw to him, but he always played as hard as he could."

In the Tulane loss, Poole received a blow that broke his jaw and cost him eight teeth. Despite the awful injury, he missed only a couple of plays. While some witnesses decried the blow as dirty football, Poole claimed it was nothing more than an accident that left "my teeth pointing toward my tonsils."

The team was an offensive powerhouse whipping Florida, Kentucky, Vanderbilt, Boston College, LSU, and Mississippi State by two touchdowns or more. The LSU game was a 49-19 romp in which seven different Rebels scored a touchdown.

One of those who didn't score was scatback Billy Mustin. Salmon kept urging him to get in on the scorefest. "Every time we would get close, [Salmon] would give [the ball] to me," Mustin recalled. "It was wearing me out. I got knocked out three times."

After that last lick, Mustin had had enough, so when he got to his feet, he trotted to the LSU sideline. A Tiger manager met him and said, "You're coming off the wrong side." Mustin replied, "If I go back over there, they are going to put me back in."

The everyday struggles and burdens of life beat us down. They may be enormous; they may be trivial with a cumulative effect. But they wear us out, so much so that we've even come up with a name for our exhaustion: chronic fatigue syndrome.

Doctors don't help too much. Sleeping pills can zonk us out; muscle relaxers can dull the weariness. Other than that, it's drag on as usual until we can collapse exhaustedly into bed.

Then along comes Jesus, as usual offering hope and relief for what ails us, though in a totally unexpected way. He says take my yoke. Whoa, there! Isn't a yoke a device for work? Exactly. Our mistake is in trying to do it all alone. Yoke ourselves to Jesus, and the power of Almighty God is at our disposal to do the heavy lifting for us.

God's strong shoulders and broad back can handle any burdens we can give him. We just have to let them go.

Losers quit when they're tired. Winners quit when they've won.
-- Author unknown

Tired and weary are a way of life
only when we fail to accept Jesus' invitation
to swap our burden for his.

DAY 28

PRESSURE COOKER

Read 1 Kings 18:16-40.

"Answer me, O Lord, answer me, so these people will know that you, O Lord, are God" (v. 37).

Because of the one-on-one, side-by-side nature of the competition, few sports can match track for the pressure it places on a runner. Except in the case of one of the most dominant runners in Ole Miss history, who felt no pressure at all.

Lee Ellis Moore wrapped up his storied career as a Rebel in June 2011 with a sixth-place finish at the NCAA Outdoor Championships. A native of Cordova, Tenn., he began running as a youngster as sort of an afterthought, something just to keep his twin brother happy. "Chase and I were pretty fast as kids and one of our friends asked if we wanted to join his team," Moore recalled. Chase did want to run and Lee went along. He has been running ever since.

Moore chose Ole Miss over Harvard and met with immediate success in Oxford in his specialty, the 400-meter hurdles, by running the fourth fastest outdoor time in school history. As a senior in 2011, he was first-team All-SEC and was honored as the conference's track and field scholar-athlete of the year. He won the SEC title in the 400 meter hurdles and was All-America.

His success put a bull's eye on his chest as the runner to beat, but he never felt any pressure -- because he never ran for himself or his own glory. He ran, instead, for someone else's glory.

REBELS

"Because I run for the sake of the name of Christ and His glory, not my own, I can say that I really don't feel any pressure," Moore said during the 2011 season. "I am not running to please men, but I seek to please my father in heaven."

Lee Ellis Moore ran wherever and at what speed his legs took him without feeling any pressure -- because he used his athletic talent as an instrument to help spread word of God's kingdom and not word of his own greatness.

You live every day with pressure. As Elijah did so long ago, you lay it on the line with everybody watching. Your family, coworkers, or employees – they depend on you. You know the pressure of a deadline, of a job evaluation, of taking the risk of asking someone to go out with you, of driving in rush-hour traffic.

Help in dealing with daily pressure is readily available, and the only price you pay for it is your willingness to believe. God will give you the grace to persevere if you ask prayerfully.

And while you may need some convincing, the pressures of daily living are really small potatoes since they all will pass. The real pressure comes when you stare into the face of eternity because what you do with it is irrevocable and forever. You can handle that pressure easily enough by deciding for Jesus. Eternity is then taken care of; the pressure's off – forever.

Pressure is for tires.

-- Charles Barkley

The greatest pressure you face in life concerns where you will spend eternity, which can be dealt with by deciding for Jesus.

KEEP OUT!

Read Exodus 26:31-35; 30:1-10.

"The curtain will separate the Holy Place from the Most Holy Place" (v. 26:33).

He wasn't even on the traveling squad and had to hitchhike to the game. When he arrived, the guards at the gate wouldn't let him into the stadium. And yet, he was the game's defensive star.

On their way to an SEC title and their second straight national championship, the Rebels of 1960 opened the season on Sept. 17 in Texas against Houston. Senior quarterback Jake Gibbs started his All-American season by throwing for three touchdowns as the Rebs waxed the Cougars 42-0. Doug Elmore passed for two, and Glynn Griffing, who would be All-America in 1962, chipped in with a scoring toss.

One of the players who wasn't on the traveling squad for the trip to Texas was junior guard Bill "Foggy" Basham. Not wanting to miss the game, he hitchhiked to Houston and arrived shortly before halftime. The guard wouldn't let him in the gate, though, so he was left standing around outside the stadium.

The Rebels were winning easily at halftime, but Houston was playing some very physical football. Six Ole Miss linemen were injured in the first half and were unable to continue, leaving head coach Johnny Vaught scrambling to put enough able bodies on the field for the last half.

Team physician Ferrell Varner knew Basham was at the gate, so he talked his way into the dressing room and told Vaught, "Foggy is here and wants to play." In desperation, Vaught agreed.

Basham played the last half and emerged as a star. On the second-half kickoff, he tackled the runner, forced a fumble, and recovered the loose football.

Of the player who couldn't even get into the stadium, Vaught said Basham "played the finest 30 minutes of football in his life."

That civic club with membership by invitation only. The bleachers where you sit while others frolic in the sky boxes. That neighborhood you can't afford a house in. You know all about being shut out of some club, some group, some place. "Exclusive" is the word that keeps you out.

The Hebrew people, too, knew about being told to keep out; only the priests could come into the presence of the holy and survive. Then along came Jesus to kick that barrier down and give us direct access to God.

In the process, though, Jesus created another exclusive club; its members are his followers, Christians, those who believe he is the Son of God and the savior of the world. This club, though, extends a membership invitation to everyone in the whole wide world; no one is excluded. Whether you're in or out depends on your response to Jesus, not on arbitrary gatekeepers.

There are clubs you can't belong to, neighborhoods you can't live in, schools you can't get into, but the roads are always open.

-- Nike

Christianity is an exclusive club, but an invitation is extended to everyone and no one is denied entry.

HAVE COURAGE

Read 1 Corinthians 16:13-14.

"Be on your guard; stand firm in the faith; be men of courage; be strong" (v. 13).

The epitaph on his grave is short, but it says much: "Chucky -- Man of Courage."

On the afternoon of Oct. 28, 1989 in the Ole Miss game against Vanderbilt, Rebel Chucky Mullins made what appeared to be a routine tackle. On the play, however, he shattered four vertebrae and was instantly paralyzed. Thus began an odyssey of tragedy and courage that transformed Mullins from a lightly recruited and relatively unknown defensive back to a nationally known symbol of grit and courage that has inspired a generation.

"After he got hurt, all Chucky could move were his lips and his eyes, but they were always smiling," recalled Billy Brewer, Chucky's head coach at the time. "He was a positive influence on everyone he encountered. He kept fighting."

Chucky fought all the way through 114 days in a Memphis hospital and four months in a rehab facility. "Unable to use his arms or legs, Chucky marched on," all the way to classes and home football games. He became friends with the heartbroken Vanderbilt player involved in the fateful play.

On the morning of May 1, 1991, though, Chucky suffered a pulmonary embolism and died five days later. He was 21.

More than two decades after his death, Chucky's courage and

inspiration remain relevant. His No. 38 was retired in 2006. Each season a player is chosen for the Chucky Mullins Courage Award and wears a special "38" patch on the shoulder. All-American Patrick Willis was the first, calling the patch a symbol of not just how we are to play, but how we are to act. Before each game, the players exit the tunnel and touch a bust of Chucky Mullins.

When we speak of courage, we often think of heroic actions such as that displayed by soldiers during wartime or firefighters during an inferno. Chucky Mullins' life demonstrates, however, that courage has another aspect.

What made his daily life courageous and admirable was not the absence of fear, which usually results from foolhardiness or a dearth of relevant information. Rather, his courage showed itself in his determined refusal to let fear and tragedy debilitate him and keep him from fighting and moving on against all odds.

This is the courage God calls upon us to demonstrate in our faith lives. When Paul urged the Christians in Corinth to "be men of courage," he wasn't telling them to rush into burning buildings. He was admonishing them to be strong and sure in their faith.

This courageous attitude is an absolute necessity for American Christians today when our faith is under attack as never before. Our spiritual courage reveals itself in our proclaiming the name of Jesus no matter what forces are arrayed against us.

Chucky Mullins epitomized courage against all odds.

-- *Billy Brewer*

To be courageous for Jesus is to speak his name boldly no matter what Satan uses against us.

MERCY ME

Read Ephesians 2:1-10.

"Because of his great love for us, God, who is rich in mercy, made us alive with Christ even when we were dead in transgressions – it is by grace you have been saved" (vv. 4-5).

The Ole Miss baseball team was not exactly feeling merciful.

The Rebels of 2001 would go 39-23, 17-13 in the SEC, and would make the program's eighth appearance in an NCAA regional. The team was tied with LSU for first place in the SEC West when it traveled to Baton Rouge for a three-game series. In the opener on April 13, LSU slammed the Rebels 15-2. The boys, therefore, were not exactly in a forgiving mood when they suited up for the second game.

Their collective disposition was not improved when the Tigers jumped out to an early 6-0 lead. The Rebel bats that had been silent all weekend suddenly came alive, though, and they stopped hitting only when they ran out of innings.

They tied the game with six runs in the third, and the score was knotted up at eight in the seventh when freshman Matt Tolbert blasted a three-run homer. After that, the Tigers could have begged for mercy and would have found none.

Showing no mercy over the last three innings, the Rebels put up 15 runs and embarrassed LSU 23-10. "Once the game turned in our favor, it just kind of snowballed," said freshman Adam

Yates, who upped his record to 5-0 with a long relief effort.

Catcher Carl Lafferty was 4-for-4, and Matt Mossberg hit his first career homer. The game got so bad for LSU that the Tiger head coach finally used his starting shortstop as his eighth pitcher to finish up.

A drunk slams into your car, hospitalizing your son. An addict burglarizes your house. Your boss gives the promotion you deserve to someone else. Your spouse walks out on you.

Somebody sometime in your life has hurt you. What's your attitude toward them? Do you scream for revenge and payback? Or do you extend mercy, showing compassion and kindness all out of proportion to what's been done to you?

Mercy is the appeal of last resort. When you are guilty, your only hope is to throw yourself upon the mercy of the court. Your only prayer is that the judge will not remorselessly hand down the sentence you deserve.

Of all God's attributes, none is more astounding than his penchant for mercy. Through Jesus, God provided the way to save us from the sentence we deserve. Through Jesus, God made his divine mercy available to us all. In so doing, though, God expects that we who avail ourselves of his mercy will show mercy toward others. We reap what we sow.

You want mercy? Go to church.

-- Wrestler 'Stone Cold' Steve Austin

**To sow mercy in our lifetimes now
is to reap mercy from God
when we stand guiltily before him.**

DAY 32

THE CHALLENGE

Read Matthew 4:12-25.

"Come, follow me," Jesus said (v. 19).

Because Ole Miss' first football players were up to a daunting challenge, the team pulled off the school's first-ever upset.

Professor Alexander Bondurant, the father of Ole Miss football, was quite concerned when his team boarded the train for the school's second-ever football game and the first one on the road. "When the train was boarded at Oxford in the gray of the morning of Nov. 18 (1893), the team was in no confident mood," Bondurant observed. "Every man realized that today he was going to be thoroughly tested."

The opposition was the Memphis Athletic Club, and the word the Oxford boys had heard about the team was not encouraging. "The center was said to be an unusual man physically, and a trained football player," Bondurant said, "and a number of the other men were former members of school and college teams."

A good contingent of fans followed the team for the first football game ever played in Memphis. Back home, a crowd gathered at Winchell and Davidson, a bookstore with a telegraph. The news they received -- to everyone's surprise -- was all good.

In the early going, however, the Mississippi boys encountered an unexpected problem when a couple of Memphis players proved adept at stealing their signals. Gradually, though, the boys' superior training had its effect. They powered their way steadily downfield until fullback William Cook scored from the four ten minutes into the game. Halfback Mordecai Jones (who scored the program's first touchdown) broke off a 60-yard touchdown run in the last half, and Ole Miss pulled off a 16-0 upset.

Facing the fledgling football program's first serious challenge, the Mississippi players had prevailed.

Like the Ole Miss athletic teams every time they take the field or the court, we are challenged daily. Life is a testing ground; God intentionally set it up that way. If we are to grow in character, confidence, and perseverance, and if we are to make a difference in the world, we must meet challenges head-on. Few things in life are as boring and as destructive to our sense of self-worth as a job that doesn't offer any challenges.

Our faith life is the same way. The moment we answered Jesus' call to "Come, follow me," we took on the most difficult challenge we will ever face. We are called to be holy by walking in Jesus' footsteps in a world that seeks to render our Lord irrelevant and his influence negligible. The challenge Jesus places before us is to put our faith and our trust in him and not in ourselves or the transitory values of the secular world.

Daily walking in Jesus' footsteps is a challenge, but the path takes us all the way right up to the gates of Heaven – and then right on through.

There was one dominant note in all that was said: 'We must beat them.'
-- Alexander Bondurant on the challenge facing his team

To accept Jesus as Lord is to joyfully take on the challenge of living a holy life in an unholy world.

UNEXPECTEDLY

Read Matthew 24:36-51.

"No one knows about that day or hour, not even the angels in heaven, nor the Son, but only the Father" (v. 36).

The Ole Miss defense had been so bad that the press used words to describe it that sent Rebel coaches scurrying to the dictionary. Thus, what the defense did to Florida was totally unexpected.

The Rebel defense entered the game of Sept. 27, 2003, against Texas Tech ranked 116th in the nation -- next to last -- in passing defense. They managed to drop a notch to dead last; Tech torched them for 661 yards passing and six touchdowns.

"I learned new words this week," said Rebel defensive coordinator Chuck Driesbach several days after the 49-45 loss. "I needed a dictionary." What he was looking up was the variety of words the press used to describe just how awful the Rebel defense was. Those same media folks were left scrambling for adjectives of a different sort after what the defense did to the Florida Gators only a week after the Tech fiasco.

With the game on the line in the fourth quarter, the Ole Miss defense limited Florida to 54 yards of total offense. The Rebs held the SEC's third-best passing attack to 51 yards in the second half and not a single completion in the fourth quarter. They also intercepted three Gator passes in the fourth quarter. Cornerback Von Hutchins and safeties Travis Blanchard and Eric Oliver nabbed the interceptions with Oliver's theft ending Florida's last threat at the Rebel 27 with 29 seconds left.

"We read and heard all the criticism," defensive tackle Jesse Mitchell said. "When you get criticized, you have to become a bigger man. I think we grew up out there today."

While the Ole Miss defense was holding Florida scoreless in the last half, tailback Vashon Pearson scored from the one with 76 seconds left to propel the Rebels to a 20-17 win. That victory wasn't necessarily unexpected; the way Ole Miss got it was.

We think we've got everything figured out and under control, and then something unexpected happens. About the only thing we can expect from life with any certainty is the unexpected.

God is that way too, suddenly showing up to remind us he's still around. A friend who calls and tells you he's praying for you, a hug from your child or grandchild, a lone lily that blooms in your yard -- unexpected moments when the divine comes crashing into our lives with such clarity that it takes our breath away and brings tears to our eyes.

But why shouldn't God do the unexpected? The only factor limiting what God can do in our lives is the paucity of our own faith. We should expect the unexpected from God, this same deity who caught everyone by surprise by unexpectedly coming to live among us as a man, and who will return when we least expect it.

For whatever reason, we were just sleeping. We woke up today.
-- Chuck Driesbach after the Florida win

God continually does the unexpected,
like showing up as Jesus,
who will return unexpectedly.

DAY 34

GIFT-WRAPPED

Read James 1:12-18.

"Every good and perfect gift is from above, coming down from the Father of the heavenly lights" (v. 17).

Ole Miss head coach Bob Weltlich had quite a birthday gift for his dad: the SEC Tournament championship.

As the 1981 SEC men's basketball tournament began in Birmingham, the Rebels were considered also-rans who didn't really have a shot. They had finished the regular season 13-13 and were the sixth seed in the tournament. As one writer put it, the Rebels were "a team headed for nowhere but Birmingham when they left Oxford."

What happened was termed Ole Miss' "Miracle on the Hardwood." The Rebs pulled off an opening-round upset with an 81-71 win over Tennessee. They then thumped Vanderbilt 71-51 to set up a championship final against Georgia and Dominique Wilkins. Interestingly, the Rebs weren't underdogs going into this one; if anything, the game was rated as dead even. In the last game of the regular season, Ole Miss had edged the Bulldogs 64-62.

Their Cinderella run appeared over, though, as Georgia ran out to a 10-point lead and held it pretty much throughout the first half. Wilkins had his way with the Rebs, scoring 20 points.

But in the last half, defensive standout Elston Turner recovered from that awful first half to outscore Wilkins and to hold him to eight points. Cinderella refused to give up her slipper.

REBELS

Turner scored six straight points to give Ole Miss a 54-53 lead with 5:43 left. The teams swapped points until Chris Barrett hit a jumper from the corner at 2:35 to push the Rebs into a 60-58 lead. They never trailed again and won 66-62.

And that birthday gift? The game was played on March 7, the 68th birthday of Weltlich's father. Happy birthday, Dad.

Receiving a gift is nice, but giving has its pleasures too, doesn't it? The children's excitement on Christmas morning. That smile of pure delight on your spouse's face when you came up with a really cool anniversary present. Your dad's surprise that time you didn't give him a tie or socks. There really does seem to be something to this being more blessed to give than to receive.

No matter how generous we may be, though, we are grumbling misers compared to God, who is the greatest gift-giver of all. That's because all the good things in our lives – every one of them – come from God. Friends, love, health, family, the air we breathe, the sun that warms us, even our very lives are all gifts from a profligate God. And here's the kicker: He even gives us eternal life with him through the gift of his son.

What in the world can we possibly give God in return? Our love and our life.

From what we get, we can make a living; what we give, however, makes a life.

– Arthur Ashe

Nobody can match God when it comes to giving, but you can give him the gift of your love in appreciation.

DAY 35

FAIL-SAFE

Read Luke 22:54-62.

"Peter remembered the word the Lord had spoken to him: 'Before the rooster crows today, you will disown me three times.' And he went outside and wept bitterly" (vv. 61b-62).

Barney Poole purposely failed two courses so he could play football for Ole Miss.

As he assembled his first Ole Miss team, head coach Johnny Vaught's initial move was to get his potential star, quarterback Charley Conerly, on board with the plan. He told Conerly, who was 24, that much would be expected of him in 1947. "You have got to stay out of honky-tonks, get yourself in shape and dedicate yourself to a fine senior year," Vaught said.

That worked out just fine. Conerly quarterbacked the Rebs to their first SEC title, led the nation in completions, was a consensus All-America, and was named one group's Player of the Year.

Vaught had another crucial situation to handle that was more problematic. End Barney Poole had been Conerly's prime target in 1942 before he went to West Point and played three seasons for the Black Knights. With World War II's end, Vaught decided he needed Poole to come back home to pair with Conerly again.

Athletic director Tad Smith realized the big problem would be getting onto the West Point grounds. So he hired a limousine to look official, and, sure enough, the gate guards waved the vehicle right on through. Despite not having any idea where to find Poole, the Ole Miss delegation happened upon him. "It was lucky that I found them," Poole recalled.

He climbed into the limousine and told Smith that he wanted to play football at Ole Miss. But Army head coach Earl Blaik had no wish to lose his All-American end, so Poole's resignation letters were refused. Finally, Poole intentionally flunked a pair of leadership courses to get out. Ole Miss gained a 23-year-old junior who was inducted into the College Football Hall of Fame in 1974.

Failure is usually defined by expectations. For instance, a baseball player who hits .300 is a star, but he fails seventy percent of the time. We grumble about a postal system that manages to deliver billions of items without a hitch.

And we are often our own harshest critics, beating ourselves up for our failings because we expected better. Never mind that our expectations were unrealistic to begin with.

The bad news about life is that failure – unlike success -- is inevitable. Only one man walked this earth perfectly and we're not him. The good news about life, however, is that failure isn't permanent. In life, we always have time to reverse our failures as did Peter, he who failed our Lord so abjectly.

The same cannot be said of death. In death we eternally suffer the consequences of our failure to follow that one perfect man.

I've failed over and over again in my life. And that is why I succeed.
                                                        -- Michael Jordan

Only one failure in life dooms us to eternal failure in death: failing to follow Jesus Christ.

DAY 36

JUGGERNAUT

Read Revelation 20.

"Fire came down from heaven and devoured them. And the devil, who deceived them, was thrown into the lake of burning sulfur, where the beast and the false prophet had been thrown" (vv. 9b-10a).

Juggernaut. That's what Mississippi State ran into head-on.

"I didn't see that one coming" was about all State head coach Sylvester Croom could say after the 2008 Egg Bowl. In perhaps the most dominating performance in the storied rivalry's long history, the Rebels slaughtered the Bulldogs 45-0. The blowout had Rebel fans late in the game throwing cotton balls down from the top of the stadium in anticipation of a Cotton Bowl bid.

Rebel head coach Houston Nutt declared that the juggernaut State ran into was primarily the defense. He had a point. What the defense pulled off was downright astounding. Rebel defenders set a school record by limiting the Bulldogs to -51 yards rushing. State was helpless on offense, managing an embarrassing total of 37 yards on 56 plays and crossing midfield just twice.

The defense set another school record with eleven sacks. End Greg Hardy had three, and tackle Peria Jerry had a pair. The State quarterbacks took a merciless beating; Jerry said he never felt sorry for them. "Quarterbacks get it easier than anybody else in practice, so when you get them in the game, you've got to make them pay," he said. They certainly paid. The anti-social defense hit State quarterbacks on nine of their first ten pass attempts., intercepted two of the first five passes, and knocked the starting quarterback out of the game twice.

Meanwhile, the offense wasn't just standing around watching the defense manhandle the Dogs. Dexter McCluster scored on a 36-yard run only 2:20 into the game. Quarterback Jevan Snead completed his first nine passes, and when he hit Mike Wallace with a 72-yard bomb in the second quarter, Ole Miss led 31-0.

"We wanted to send a message," Snead said. State heard it.

Maybe your experience with a juggernaut involved a game against a team full of major college prospects, a league tennis match against a former college player, or your presentation for the project you knew didn't stand a chance. Whatever it was, you've been slam-dunked before.

Being part of a juggernaut is certainly more fun than being in the way of one. Just ask State in 2008. Or consider the forces of evil aligned against God. At least when the Bulldogs took the field against the Rebs in 2008, they had some hope that they might win. No such hope exists for those who oppose God.

That's because their fate is already spelled out in detail. It's in the book; we all know how the story ends. God's enemies may talk big and bluster now, but they will be soundly trounced and routed in the most decisive defeat of all time.

Total domination.

-- Houston Nutt on the 2008 Egg Bowl

**The most lopsided victory in all of history is a
sure thing: God's ultimate triumph over evil.**

PAYBACK

Read Matthew 5:38-42.

*"I tell you, Do not resist an evil person. If someone strikes
you on the right cheek, turn to him the other also" (v. 39).*

The '59 Rebels exacted some sweet revenge, and in the process
they won the school's first-ever national championship.

Ole Miss was ranked No. 3 in the country, and LSU was No. 1
when the teams met on Halloween night 1959 in what remains
one of the greatest college football games ever played. Robert
Khayat, who would later serve as the Ole Miss chancellor, booted
a 22-yard field goal in the first quarter for a 3-0 Rebel lead.

After that, Ole Miss played field position and let its defense
pound on the hapless LSU offense. That worked until All-American Billy Cannon returned a punt 89 yards for the game-winning
touchdown. The final score was 7-3. Said Rebel quarterback Jake
Gibbs, "I've never seen a bunch of grown men cry like babies as I
did that night in our dressing room. Man, that game hurt."

But all was far from over for Ole Miss. Disappointed but refusing to fold, the Rebs ran the table to finish 9-1. When Tennessee
upset LSU by a point and the Tigers also finished 9-1, sentiment
arose across the South for a rematch. The Sugar Bowl obliged.

Thus, on Jan. 1, 1960, the Rebels had a shot at payback -- and took
it. As it had in the first game, the Rebel defense totally dominated
the LSU offense, holding the Tigers to -15 yards rushing; Cannon
could manage but 8 yards. Senior linebacker Larry Grantham "hit

Cannon every time he moved that day," Gibbs said.

On offense, senior quarterback Bobby Franklin, who was the game's MVP, threw for two touchdowns and Gibbs threw for another.

Ole Miss had its revenge with a 21-0 whipping of the Tigers. Three different polls named the Rebs national champions.

The very nature of an intense rivalry such as that of Ole Miss and LSU requires that the loser seek payback for the defeat of the season before. But what about in life when somebody's done you wrong; is it time to get even?

The problem with revenge in real-life is that it isn't as clear-cut as a scoreboard. Life is so messy that any attempt at revenge is often inadequate or, worse, backfires and injures you.

As a result, you remain gripped by resentment and anger, which hurts you and no one else. You poison your own happiness while that other person goes blithely about her business. The only way someone who has hurt you can keep hurting you is if you're a willing participant.

But it doesn't have to be that way. Jesus ushered in a new way of living when he taught that we are not to seek revenge for personal wrongs and injuries. Let it go and go on with your life. What a relief!

It was unbelievable. Everything was working.
-- Bobby Franklin on the 1960 Sugar Bowl

Resentment and anger over a wrong injures you,
not the other person, so forget it
-- just as Jesus taught.

DAY 38

KEEPING THE PEACE

Read Hebrews 12:14-17.

"Make every effort to live in peace with all men and to be holy" (v. 14).

A post-game brawl led to the creation of what may well be the most beautiful trophy in college football.

In 1926, Ole Miss beat Mississippi A&M 7-6. Three pass completions from quarterback Harvey Walker powered a second-quarter drive that ended with a 3-yard TD from fullback Lacey Biles. Ole Miss captain Webster Burke, who was suffering from a jammed toe, booted his first extra-point attempt of the season. It was the only extra point he ever made in college. It also turned out to be the game winner when A&M scored but missed the extra point because of a good rush from the Ole Miss line.

Exuberant Mississippi fans rushed "like madmen onto the field" with one aim in mind: to pull down the goalposts. As the A&M yearbook later put it, "that was entirely the wrong attitude," and "a few chairs had to be sacrificed over the heads" of the would-be vandals. A full-scale brawl broke out as A&M fans and students "defended their honor with weapons including cane-bottom chairs." History records that the players on both sides stayed out of the melee. The goal posts were saved.

Not surprisingly, though, Ole Miss fans didn't take kindly to being clobbered over the head with chairs. What became known as "The Battle of Starkville" thus continued long after the game.

REBELS

In an effort to prevent future violence, shocked officials from both schools suggested shipping the goalposts to the winning team each year with the winner footing the bill. That was deemed too impractical. Late in 1926, student delegations came up with a plan for a football-shaped trophy to be presented in a "dignified" post-game ceremony and held for a year by the winning team.

Out of a brawl, the famous Golden Egg was born.

Perhaps you've never been in a brawl or a public brouhaha to match that of 1926's "Battle of Starkville." But maybe you retaliated when you got one elbow too many in a pickup basketball game. Or maybe you and your spouse or your teenager get into it occasionally, shouting and saying cruel things. Or road rage may be a part of your life.

While we do seem to live in a more belligerent, confrontational society than ever before, fighting is still not the solution to a problem. Rather, it only escalates the whole confrontation, leaving wounded pride, intransigence, and simmering hatred in its wake. Actively seeking and making peace is the way to a solution that lasts and heals broken relationships and aching hearts.

Peacemaking is not as easy as fighting, but it is much more courageous and a lot less painful. It is also exactly what Jesus would do.

Aggie fans responded to the Ole Miss celebration with malice afore-thought with the intent of staging a free for all.
> -- The Mississippian *on the 'Battle of Starkville'*

**Making peace instead of fighting takes courage
and strength; it's also what Jesus would do.**

HERO WORSHIP

Read 1 Samuel 16:1-13.

*"Do not consider his appearance or his height, for . . . the
Lord does not look at the things man looks at. . . . The
Lord looks at the heart" (v. 7).*

The smallest man on the floor was the biggest hero of the night,
making what was called "arguably the biggest basket in Ole Miss
history."

Jason Harrison stood only 5-5 when he played for the Rebels
from 1998-2002. All-SEC as a junior point guard, Harrison is one
of two players in University history with 1,000 points and 400
assists. (Former head coach Rod Barnes is the other.) He is third
in Rebel history for both steals and assists in a career.

The Rebels of 2000-01 were Western Division champions and
advanced to the finals of the SEC Tournament before losing. They
then nipped Iona 72-70 in the first round of the NCAA Tournament, which set up a game with Notre Dame for a shot at the first
berth in the Sweet 16 in school history.

What resulted was called "a great college basketball game"
by the Irish head coach -- and he was on the losing end, thanks
largely to Harrison's heroics.

It may have been a great game, but it wasn't necessarily a very
pretty one. The Rebels hit only 3 of 16 3-point shots while their
defense held Notre Dame to 29 percent shooting. On the pretty
side, though, All-American Rahim Lockhart poured in 24 points

for the Rebels. And then there was Harrison's shot, which was certainly a thing of beauty.

Notre Dame led 55-54 and the shot clock was winding down when Harrison launched a 23-foot bomb that exploded in Notre Dame's face with 46 seconds left. That sealed the 59-56 win.

"The little man did it again," said guard Jason Flanigan. "We hadn't made outside shots all day, but Jason knocked down the one we needed most." Just being a hero, that's all.

Athletes are heroes when they play at their best when the game is on the line. More generally, a hero is commonly thought of as someone who performs brave and dangerous feats that save or protect someone's life. You figure that excludes you.

But ask your son about that when you show him how to bait a hook, or your daughter when you show up for her dance recital. Look into the eyes of those Little Leaguers you help coach.

Ask God about heroism when you're steady in your faith. For God, a hero is a person with the heart of a servant. And if a hero is a servant who acts to save other's lives, then the greatest hero of all is Jesus Christ.

God seeks heroes today, those who will proclaim the name of their hero – Jesus – proudly and boldly, no matter how others may scoff or ridicule. God knows heroes when he sees them -- by what's in their hearts.

They just made more plays at crunch time than we did.
       -- Irish head coach Mike Brey describing the Rebs' late heroics

**God's heroes are those who remain steady
in their faith while serving others.**

ONE-MAN ARMY

Read Revelation 19:11-21.

"The rest of them were killed by the sword that came out
of the mouth of the rider on the horse" (v. 21).

Senior Rebel fullback Arnold "Showboat" Boykin was a one-man army against Mississippi State in 1951, accomplishing a feat that had never been done in college football.

Boykin spent much of his time at Ole Miss injured. As a senior in 1951, he had scored only three touchdowns all season when the 5-3-1 Rebels met the 4-4 Mississippi State Bulldogs on Dec. 1 in Starkville. The Rebels thrashed State 49-7, which was something of a surprise. An even bigger surprise, however, was that Boykin scored all seven of the Ole Miss touchdowns, an NCAA record that stood until 1990. His 42 points was also a collegiate record, broken by Syracuse's legendary Jim Brown in 1956.

On the fifth play of the game at the State 21, Boykin went "side-wheeling through the line" for his first score. His second TD was a 14-yard run; his third, still in the first quarter, was a 12-yard scamper. At halftime, Ole Miss led 28-7, and Boykin had racked up his fourth touchdown, another 14-yard run.

On the third Rebel play of the last half, Boykin ripped off his longest run of the day, racing 85 yards down the sideline for his fifth touchdown. He broke the SEC record with his sixth score midway through the fourth quarter, this one covering one yard. His final score came late in the game, a 5-yard touchdown run.

Interestingly, all of Boykin's scores come on the same play, a simple trap handoff from quarterback Jimmy Lear. The play's success was the brainstorm of tackle Kline Gilbert. Early in the game, he suggested to guard and team captain Othar Crawford that they change their assignments to give Crawford a better blocking angle. State never adjusted to the change.

Arnold "Showboat" Boykin was a one-man army against Mississippi State in 1951, but the win belonged to the whole team. A similar situation will occur when Christ returns. He will not come back to us as the meek lamb led unprotestingly to slaughter on the cross. Instead, he will be a one-man army, a rider on a white horse who will destroy those forces responsible for disorder and chaos in God's world.

This image of our Jesus as a warrior may well shock and discomfort us; it should also excite and thrill us. It reminds us vividly that God will unleash his awesome power to effect justice and righteousness in a world that persecutes his people and slanders his name. It should also lend us a sense of urgency because the time will pass when decisions for Christ can still be made.

For now, Jesus has an army at his disposal in the billions of Christians around the world. We are Christian soldiers; we have a world to conquer for our Lord – before he returns as a one-man army to finish the job.

I never did keep count, but I remember Jimmy Lear saying, 'We'll try you again.' It kept working.
*   -- Arnold Boykin on his record-setting game*

**Jesus will return as a one-man army to conquer
the forces of evil; for now, we are his army.**

PARTY ANIMALS

Read Exodus 14:26-31; 15:19-21.

"Miriam the prophetess, Aaron's sister, took a tambourine in her hand, and all the women followed her, with tambourines and dancing" (v. 15:20).

The Crimson Tide threw a great big old party. They just invited the wrong guests to their shebang.

On Oct. 8, 1988, the 12th-ranked Tide celebrated homecoming at Bryant-Denny Stadium. The faithful also gathered to applaud themselves with the grand opening of the new Paul (Bear) Bryant Museum. Their homecoming sacrifice *du jour* was Ole Miss.

The Rebs were a likely choice not to spoil the party. They were 18-point underdogs and were 0-14 in Tuscaloosa. They were also coming off a bad season in 1987 thanks primarily to NCAA sanctions. As head coach Billy Brewer put it, "Everybody was questioning everybody from the coaches to the guy who parked the cars. . . . I felt like we were having to start over (in 1988)."

Nothing about the party went as Alabama had planned. The first half was certainly not a joyous occasion; it ended scoreless. When the Tide returned the second-half kickoff 100 yards for a touchdown and followed that up with a safety and a field goal for a 12-0 lead, it seemed as though the players had simply arrived a little late for their own party.

But tailback Shawn Sykes crashed the party with a 53-yard touchdown run with 5:26 to go in the third. Then on third and 10

REBELS

at the Alabama 12 with only 46 seconds to play, Rebel offensive coordinator Red Parker surprised everybody -- especially the Alabama defense -- by calling a quick hitter up the middle. On only his third carry of the game, Sykes scored his second touchdown. Darron Billings' run on the conversion made it 15-12.

After an Alabama fumble, fullback Joe Mickles navigated 18 yards for a touchdown that wrapped up the 22-12 Ole Miss win. It also turned out the lights; this party was over.

You know what it takes to throw a good party. You start with your closest friends, add some salsa and chips, fire up the grill and throw on some burgers and dogs, and then top it all off with the Ole Miss game on TV. You also know that any old half-decent excuse will do to get people together for a celebration. All you really need is a sense that life is pretty good right now.

That's the thing about having Jesus as part of your life: He turns every day into a celebration of the good life. No matter what tragedies or setbacks life may have in store – and they will come -- the heart given to Jesus will find the joy in living. That's because such a life is spent with quiet confidence in God's promise of salvation through Jesus, a confidence that inevitably bubbles up into a joy the troubles of the world cannot touch. When a life is celebrated with Jesus, the party never stops.

After the game, Ole Miss coach Billy Brewer and his players stayed out on the field to soak up the celebration mood.
– Description of Ole Miss' postgame party in Tuscaloosa

With Jesus, life is one big party because it becomes a celebration of victory and joy.

PRACTICE SESSION

Read 2 Peter 1:3-11.

"For if you do these things, you will never fail, and you will receive a rich welcome into the eternal kingdom of our Lord and Savior Jesus Christ" (vv. 10b-11).

Apparently the old adage that practice makes perfect never applied to Ole Miss guard/forward Ken Turner.

Turner played for the Rebs from 1967-69. His senior season he averaged 15.9 points per game, 20.5 points per game in SEC play. He was honorable mention All-SEC in '68 and third team in '69.

He played during the Pete Maravich era, which meant he, like almost everybody else in the league, was overshadowed by the Pistol. On March 1, 1969, in the last home game of the season, however, Turner stole the spotlight from Maravich. Oh, the Pistol had a pretty good game, all right; he scored 49 points. But in the closing seconds of the game when the outcome was decided, it was Turner and not Maravich who made the difference.

The Rebels jumped out to a 10-point lead in the first half before falling behind by seven with only seven minutes left. Over the next five minutes, though, Ole Miss put together a rally that tied the game at 76. With 2:04 left, LSU held the ball for the sure game-winning shot Maravich would take. Rebel center Jerry Brawner intercepted a pass, though, giving the Rebs a shot at the last shot.

They set up a play for Turner, and with only two seconds left, he hit it for the 78-76 win. He led the Rebel scoring with 28 points while Brawner had 17 points and led all rebounders with 21. Ron Coleman also dropped in 17 points.

Except for the game-winning shot, it was not an especially exceptional game by Turner's high standards. What made it exceptional, however, is that he hadn't practiced a lick all week. He had been sidelined by an illness.

Imagine a football team that never practices. A play cast that doesn't rehearse. A preacher who never reviews or practices his sermon beforehand. When the showdown comes, they would be revealed as inept bumblers that merit our disdain.

We practice something so that we will become good at it, so that it becomes so natural that we can pull it off without even having to think about it. Interestingly, if we are to live as Christ wants us to, then we must practice that lifestyle – and showing up at church and sitting stoically on a pew once a week does not constitute practice. To practice successfully, we must participate; we must do repeatedly whatever it is we want to be good at.

We must practice being like Christ by living like Christ every day of our lives. For Christians, practice is a lifestyle that doesn't make perfect -- only Christ is perfect – but it does prepare us for the real thing: the day we meet God face to face and inherit Christ's kingdom.

You play like you practice and you practice like you play.
-- Former Virginia head football coach George Welsh

Practicing the Christian lifestyle doesn't
make us perfect, but it does secure us
a permanent place beside the perfect one.

CONFIDENCE MAN

Read Micah 7:5-7.

"As for me, I will look to the Lord, I will wait for the God of my salvation" (v. 7 NRSV).

With his first game as the Rebel head football coach nearing, Harry Mehre had his boys confident they could win. Good thing they were unaware he didn't exactly share their confidence.

After his first talk with the Ole Miss search committee following the 1937 season, Mehre's assessment was that the Rebel football program was in a mess. The head of the committee agreed. "We were dragging pretty low," said Dr. T.A. Bickerstaff. "We were not in a very good position." To change everything, the committee reviewed fifty coaches before finally deciding on Mehre, who had been let go after ten seasons as the head coach at Georgia.

Mehre faced quite a challenge. He had to take the shortage of talent that returned from a team that had lost five times in 1937 and teach it the Notre Dame box offense he had learned playing for Knute Rockne.

But Mehre also had to instill some confidence in his players. That was another problem entirely, since the opening game of 1938 was on the road against LSU, which had whipped the Rebs 13-0 each of the last two seasons. Thus, Mehre preached that his team could whip the Tigers. LSU doesn't have "anything over you that hard work and dedication can't overcome.... The only way to have an undefeated season is to win the first one," he exhorted.

REBELS

The players bought it, in the process becoming more confident than their head coach, who privately fretted. "LSU for an opener. Well, we can't forfeit," he said. "The game is there; it is up to us to make the best of it."

The confident Rebels did just that. Led by senior All-American Parker Hall, who threw a touchdown pass to Ham Murphy and returned an LSU punt to the one, Ole Miss won 20-7.

You need confidence in all areas of your life. You're confident the company you work for will pay you on time, or you wouldn't go to work. You turn the ignition confident your car will start. When you flip a switch, you expect the light to come on.

Confidence in other people and in things is often misplaced, though. Companies go broke; car batteries die; light bulbs burn out. Even the people you love the most sometimes let you down.

So where can you place your trust with absolute confidence you won't be betrayed? In the promises of God.

Such confidence is easy, of course, when everything's going your way, but what about when you cry as Micah did, "What misery is mine!" That's when your confidence in God must be its strongest. That's when you wait for the Lord confident that God will not fail you, that he will never let you down.

I truly wish I had a camera. I don't know how this game will turn out, but the scoreboard shows us ahead of LSU, 7 to 0.
-- A less-than-confident Dr. T.A. Bickerstaff after Ole Miss scored first

People, things, and organizations
will let you down; only God can be trusted
absolutely and confidently.

IN GOD'S OWN TIME

Read James 5:7-12.

"Be patient, then, brothers, until the Lord's coming" (v. 7).

Most players wait only a few months to begin playing ball for the team they commit to in high school. Jerrell Powe waited more than three years.

Powe finished his career at Ole Miss in 2010 as a team captain and a two-year starter at nose tackle. He was second-team All-SEC as a junior and as a senior and was taken in the sixth round of the 2011 NFL draft by the Kansas City Chiefs. He reached the NFL only after years of patience and determination.

Powe was a five-star recruit when he signed with Ole Miss in 2005. The NCAA declared him academically ineligible, however, because he did not meet the core courses requirement. In August, he enrolled at Hargrove Military Academy in Virginia.

In February 2006, Powe signed a second letter of intent to play at Ole Miss. In August, though, as football practice was to begin, the NCAA struck again, ruling him ineligible because he had received too much help in completing his coursework.

Powe took the NCAA to court and was admitted to Ole Miss in the fall of 2006 but could not take part in football. He could only wait. "I'm not going to give up now. I went too far," he said.

He needed that patience. In August 2007, Powe signed a third letter of intent at Ole Miss, but incredibly, the NCAA ruled him ineligible again. He was allowed to receive a football scholarship but could not play or practice until the fall of 2008. Finally, on July 28, 2008, only days before practice began and after Powe had established a 2.3 GPA, he was ruled eligible to play.

As Powe began his junior season in 2009, the reality of his long journey hit home: His football contemporaries had already completed their eligibility and been drafted by the NFL.

Have you ever left a restaurant because the server didn't take your order quickly enough? Complained at your doctor's office about how long you had to wait? Wondered how much longer a sermon was going to last?

It isn't just the machinations of the world with which we're impatient; we want God to move at our pace, not his. For instance, how often have you prayed and expected – indeed, demanded – an immediate answer from God? And aren't Christians the world over impatient for the glorious day when Jesus will return and set everything right? We're in a hurry, but God obviously isn't.

As rare as it seems to be, patience is nevertheless included among the likes of gentleness, humility, kindness, and compassion as attributes of a Christian.

God expects us to be patient. He knows what he's doing, he is in control, and his will shall be done. On his schedule, not ours.

Every now and then, I pat myself on the back. It was a long road, a lot of heartbreak.
                                        -- Jerrell Powe on finally playing for Ole Miss

God moves in his own time, so often we must wait for him to act, remaining faithful and patient.

DAY 45

TIME FOR A CHANGE

Read Romans 6:1-14.

"Just as Christ was raised from the dead through the glory of the Father, we too may live a new life" (v. 4).

The so-called experts said Ole Miss' SEC title in 1947 was a fluke, that they would settle back into their status as an also-ran. But that was before Johnny Vaught unleashed a big change on the rest of the league.

When he took over as Rebel head coach in 1947, Vaught toyed with "springing the Split-T [offense] on the South." He decided not to make the move, though, so he could utilize Charley Conerly's special talents, especially his passing ability. With the 1948 season and Conerly gone to the pros, however, the time had come for a change. The offense was perfect for the type of players Vaught had: speedy backs and small and undermanned linemen.

The biggest problem was finding the right quarterback, and six Rebels got a shot during the spring. The unlikeliest one of all became the first Split-T quarterback in the South. A halfback the season before, Farley "Fish" Salmon wasn't even sure he would come out for football his senior year. But the Split-T intrigued him, and he decided to give it a shot.

The problem was he stood only 5-8 and weighed 145 pounds, not exactly the physical attributes Vaught wanted in his offensive leader. "Coach Vaught never could accept the fact I was the No. 1 quarterback," Salmon said. Even after Salmon won the job in the spring, Vaught kept looking, demoting Salmon to third team in the fall.

But Salmon was the man. His speed, plus that of running backs Dixie Howell, Bobby Wilson, Jerry Tiblier, and Billy Mustin, was a perfect complement to the small, quick linemen up front. With the change in the offense, the '48 squad went 8-1, losing only to Tulane while rolling up 226 points. Salmon was All-SEC; senior split end Barney Poole was All-America for the third time.

Anyone who asserts no change is needed in his or her life just isn't paying attention. Every life has doubt, worry, fear, failure, frustration, unfulfilled dreams, and unsuccessful relationships in some combination. The memory and consequences of our past often haunt and trouble us.

Recognizing the need for change in our lives, though, doesn't mean the changes that will bring about hope, joy, peace, and fulfillment will occur. We need some power greater than ourselves or we wouldn't be where we are.

So where can we turn? Where lies the hope for a changed life? It lies in an encounter with the Lord of all Hope: Jesus Christ. For a life turned over to Jesus, change is inevitable. With Jesus in charge, the old self with its painful and destructive ways of thinking, feeling, loving, and living is transformed.

A changed life is always only a talk with Jesus away.

Change is an essential element of sports, as it is of life.
-- *Erik Brady,* USA Today

**In Jesus lie the hope and the power
that change lives.**

JUST PERFECT

Read Matthew 5:43-48.

"Be perfect, therefore, as your heavenly Father is perfect"
(v. 48).

If you're going to beat the defending champions in the NCAA
Tournament, a team you've already lost to by 31 points, you need
to play some perfect basketball. The Rebels did for about ten minutes -- and that was enough.

Carol Ross' Rebels were 22-10 when they met Maryland in the
second round of the 2007 tournament. They had looked solid in
beating TCU 88-74 in the first round. The Terps were a different
matter, however. They were the defending national champions,
and with all five starters back, they were the odds-on favorite to
claim the championship again. What's more, they had routed the
Rebels 110-79 early in the season.

Interestingly, before the game, Ross told her Rebs that if they
tried to play a perfect game, they would lose. "Every pretty game
we've had, trying to make everything perfect, we've always lost,"
said senior forward Jada Mincy. So Ole Miss went right out and
pulled off a 10-minute span that was indeed about as perfect as a
basketball team could play.

Maryland went up 6-2 as play started. But then "Mississippi
put on a defensive display for the ages." The Rebs ripped off ten
unanswered points, having forced six turnovers in four minutes.
A Maryland time out born of desperation merely interrupted the

run; it certainly didn't end it. When Rebel All-American point guard Armintie Price sliced through the Terp defense for another layup with eight minutes left in the first half, Ole Miss led 35-12. They had outscored Maryland 33-6.

Ross said of that ten-minute span of perfect Rebel basketball: "We jumped them, we throttled them." And they won 89-78.

Nobody's perfect; we all make mistakes every day. We botch our personal relationships; at work we seek competence, not perfection. To insist upon personal or professional perfection in our lives is to establish an impossibly high standard that will eventually destroy us physically, emotionally, and mentally.

Yet that is exactly the standard God sets for us. Our love is to be perfect, never ceasing, never failing, never qualified – just the way God loves us. And Jesus didn't limit his command to only preachers and goody-two-shoes types. All of his disciples are to be perfect as they navigate their way through the world's ambiguous definition and understanding of love.

But that's impossible! Well, not necessarily, if to love perfectly is to serve God wholeheartedly and to follow Jesus with single-minded devotion. Anyhow, in his perfect love for us, God makes allowance for our imperfect love and the consequences of it in the perfection of Jesus.

If we chase perfection, we can catch excellence.

-- Vince Lombardi

In his perfect love for us, God provides a way for us to escape the consequences of our imperfect love for him: Jesus.

DAY 47

A LONG SHOT

Read Matthew 9:9-13.

"[Jesus] saw a man named Matthew sitting at the tax collector's booth. 'Follow me,' he told him, and Matthew got up and followed him" (v. 9).

The Rebels were something of a long shot against the Texas Tech Red Raiders in the 1998 Independence Bowl.

Under normal circumstances, the Rebs would probably have been underdogs to the boys from Lubbock anyhow -- but these were anything but normal circumstances for the boys from Oxford. They were, in fact, chaotic times.

As the season ended with three straight losses, rumors swirled that head coach Tommy Tuberville had cut a deal with Auburn. He denied them and then one day after the Egg Bowl signed a contract with the Tigers. "Rebel fans were furious."

Longtime Tennessee assistant David Cutcliffe was named the new head Rebel on Dec. 2, which barely gave him enough time to learn the players' names before the bowl game on Dec. 31. His situation was complicated by an attack of pancreatitis that landed him in a hospital for five days the week before the game. The doctors said he wouldn't be well enough to join the team.

And then there was the status of sophomore quarterback Romaro Miller, who had suffered a collarbone injury that sidelined him late in the season. Even if he were able to play, how effective would he be?

Amidst all that uncertainty the Rebels had to go out and play a pretty good football team.

But Cutcliffe made it to Shreveport, Miller rewrote the bowl game's record books with three touchdown passes, and the long shots won 35-18 with a fourth-quarter explosion. Aware of their new coach's recent illness, the players dumped a cooler full of paper cups on him rather than the usual ice-cold liquid.

Matthew the tax collector was another long shot, an unlikely person to be a confidant of the Son of God. While we may not get all warm and fuzzy about the IRS, our government's revenue agents are nothing like Matthew and his ilk. He bought a franchise, paying the Roman Empire for the privilege of extorting, bullying, and stealing everything he could from his own people. Tax collectors of the time were "despicable, vile, unprincipled scoundrels."

And yet, Jesus said only two words to this lowlife: "Follow me." Jesus knew that this long shot would make an excellent disciple.

It's the same with us. While we may not be quite as vile as Matthew was, none of us can stand before God with our hands clean and our hearts pure. We are all impossibly long shots to enter God's Heaven. That is, until we do what Matthew did: get up and follow Jesus.

I've never been so proud of a football team as I am of you guys tonight.
-- David Cutcliffe after his long shots won the Independence Bowl

**Only through Jesus does our status change
from being long shots to enter God's Kingdom
to being heavy favorites.**

DAY 48

THE MOTHER LODE

Read John 19:25-30.

"Near the cross of Jesus stood his mother" (v. 25).

Peria and John Jerry didn't have time for football -- and then their mother stepped in.

Growing up on a Mississippi farm, the brothers had chores to do. Their father insisted that their time be devoted to feeding the horses and the goats, bringing in the hay, gathering the eggs, and cleaning barnyards -- not to anything as useless as sports. But Onethia Jerry stepped in and changed the boys' lives forever.

She took care of their chores, freeing them for football. "Everything that they had to do, I did it," she said. Dad worked late at night, so when he came home, he always found that the checklist of the boys' chores was complete. "While I was cutting the grass, I would go in and out of the house cooking," mama remembered.

The Jerry boys hit the football field, "transforming from 'wild boys' with limitless energy into athletic and graceful men." Their mother managed to keep their secret from the boys' father while they played junior high football. Once they entered high school, though, they were stars and were secrets no longer. Dad worked so he didn't attend games, but he always listened on the radio.

Not that all that work on the farm was bad for the boys. They grew into giants with prodigious strength, the latter the result of tossing hay bales and wrestling pigs in the mud. They rode wild horses and grew up tough. "They'd get hurt, thrown into barb wire, and they'd sit there and laugh," their mother recalled.

Both Peria and John went on to star for the Rebels. Peria was an All-America defensive tackle who was taken in the first round of the 2009 draft by the Atlanta Falcons. John was an offensive guard taken in the 2010 draft by the Miami Dolphins.

They remembered what their mother had done for them, telling her while they were at Ole Miss that before too long, when they turned pro, she'd be able to sit down, her work done.

Mamas often sacrifice for their children as Onethia Jerry did for her sons. No mother in history, though, has faced a challenge to match that of Mary, whom God chose to be the mother of Jesus. Like mamas and their children throughout time, Mary experienced both joy and perplexity in her relationship with her son.

To the end, though, Mary stood by her boy. She followed him all the way to his execution, an act of love and bravery since Jesus was condemned as an enemy of the Roman Empire.

But just as mothers like Mary and Onethia Jerry -- and perhaps yours -- would apparently do anything for their children, so will God do anything out of love for his children. After all, that was God on the cross at the foot of which Mary stood, and he was dying for you, one of his children.

'When I get big I'm going to buy you ten pairs of shoes.' 'I'm going to get you ten pair, too.'
– Little boys Peria and John Jerry to their mother

Mamas often sacrifice for their children,
but God, too, will do anything out of love
for his children, including dying on a cross.

DAY 49

THE PANIC BUTTON

Read Mark 4:35-41.

"He said to his disciples, 'Why are you so afraid? Do you still have no faith?'" (v. 40).

It might have been a good time for the Ole Miss basketball team to panic. Instead, they followed the example of their unflappable point guard, Chris Warren, and rallied for a big win.

Of the regular-season finale on the road against Arkansas on March 6, 2010, one sportswriter penned, "To be frank, it looked like this Ole Miss basketball team had no shot to win the game with about five minutes left." That's when full-blown panic mode was perhaps called for. After all, this was a very big game for the Rebs; a win meant a share of the SEC's Western Division title.

But as the clock ticked under the five-minute mark, the Rebs trailed by nine and appeared to be going nowhere -- except home. But they didn't panic. Head coach Andy Kennedy said it was for a good reason: They were used to such situations. Indeed, it was the fourth time in SEC play that season the Rebels found themselves behind by double digits in the last half and rallied to win. And that's what they did this time too. They won 68-66.

"I saw a team that didn't give in," Kennedy said. He also saw a team that kept its cool. Especially Warren. "That dude is just ice cold," said a laughing teammate, Trevor Gaskins, after the game. "In any basketball game, you have to have guys on your team step up and make plays to win," Warren said with his customary aplomb. "That's what I try to do. No big secret."

The "ice-cold dude" poured in 31 points, including the go-ahead 3-pointer with 53 seconds left to pace the last-gasp comeback. Just cool, calm, and collected. And a big win.

Have you ever experienced that suffocating sensation of fear escalating into full-blown panic? Maybe the time when you couldn't find your child at the mall or at the beach? Or the heart-stopping moment when you looked out and saw that tornado headed your way?

As the disciples illustrate, the problem with panic is that it debilitates us. Here they were, some professional fishermen in the bunch, and they let a bad storm panic them into helplessness. All they could do was wake up an exhausted Jesus.

We shouldn't be too hard on them, though, because we often make an even more grievous mistake. They panicked and turned to Jesus; we panic and often turn away from Jesus by underestimating both his power and his ability to handle our crises.

We have a choice when fear clutches us: We can assume Jesus no longer cares for us, surrender to it, and descend into panic, or we can remember how much Jesus loves us and resist fear and panic by trusting in him.

We've been behind in these situations as much as any team I've ever been a part of, and we continue to battle.
-- Andy Kennedy on how his team didn't panic

To plunge into panic is to believe
– quite wrongly -- that Jesus is incapable
of handling the crises in our lives.

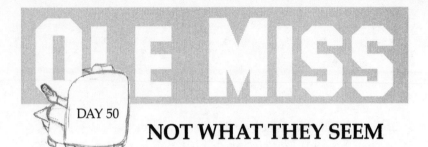

NOT WHAT THEY SEEM

Read Habakkuk 1:2-11.

"Why do you make me look at injustice? Why do you tolerate wrong? Destruction and violence are before me; there is strife, and conflict abounds" (v. 3).

How in the world could a Latin and Greek scholar with absolutely no football experience at all coach the first Ole Miss team to a 4-1 record? Well, things weren't exactly as they seemed.

The official records list Professor Alexander Bondurant as the first-ever Mississippi head football coach. The young Latin and Greek teacher did indeed lead the drive to start a football program at the school in 1893. (See Devotion No. 1.) When his efforts met with an enthusiastic response from the students, Bondurant realized that he didn't know enough to teach them football. So he proceeded to seek some help.

He sent letters to several colleges asking for assistance. James W.S. Rhea of Memphis answered the call. He had played football at Hampden-Sydney, which was also Bondurant's alma mater. He had just started a boys' prep school, but was too fascinated by football to resist Bondurant's plea. Thus, he took a train down to Oxford, and an hour after he arrived, "he had the team surging in conflict" as he taught them about the flying wedge and the like.

Rhea's efforts were purely voluntary. "There was no money to employ a regular coach," Bondurant recalled. Still, the 24-year-old came down several times and spent a day or two each trip teaching the would-be football players the basics of the game.

When Rhea returned to Memphis after a weekend of coaching his first trip, he left Bondurant with a set of instructions for practice to get them ready for the first game. That occurred on Nov. 11, 1893, a 56-0 stomping of Southwestern Baptist University. One of the oddities of the game was that Rhea was an official.

Thus, on paper, a university classics professor was the coach, but in reality a man from Memphis did the real coaching.

Sometimes in life things aren't what they seem. In our violent and convulsive times, we must confront the possibility of a new reality: that we are helpless in the face of anarchy; that injustice, destruction, and violence are pandemic in and symptomatic of our modern age. Anarchy seems to be winning, and the system of standards, values, and institutions we have cherished appears to be crumbling while we watch.

But we should not be deceived or disheartened. God is, in fact, the arch-enemy of chaos, the creator of order and goodness, and the architect of all of history. God is in control. We often misinterpret history as the record of mankind's accomplishments -- which it isn't -- rather than the unfolding of God's plan -- which it is. That plan has a clearly defined end: God will make everything right. In that day things will be what they seem.

Nothing is ever as good as it seems or as bad as it seems.
-- Former Clemson coach Curley Hallman

The forces of good and decency often seem
helpless before evil's power, but don't be fooled:
God is in control and will set things right.

THE GOOD OLD DAYS

Read Psalm 102.

"My days vanish like smoke; . . . but you remain the same, and your years will never end" (vv. 3, 27).

They remain the good old days, a time when everyone associated with them knew they were special. They were the years from 1958-62 when Ole Miss and LSU met in college football's greatest and most important rivalry.

The game was played against a backdrop of a more innocent time. Think *Happy Days*, Friday night bonfires, pep rallies, and a guy's best girl wearing his 'M' letter sweater. Ole Miss was in a dry county, so enterprising students frequently drove the thirty miles to Holly Springs to buy adult beverages.

And then there was the football and a rivalry like no other in either school's history. From 1958-62, both teams were ranked in the top 10 in five of the six games played. (They played twice in '59.) What had heretofore been pretty much a sectional rivalry of next-door neighbors became "nail-biting, dramatic battles for national rankings, conference championships and bowl games."

"It was hard-nosed football," recalled Jake Gibbs, who quarterbacked the Rebels from 1958-60. "But it was clean football, just a lot of fun. Both teams had a lot of respect for each other, and a lot of us are still friends to this day."

It was a time of psychological ploys. Most of the games were played in Tiger Stadium, which Rebel head coach Johnny Vaught

REBELS

preferred because Ole Miss got half the gate receipts. But Vaught had the problem of convincing his players that Tiger Stadium was friendly territory. One year, as his young team waited anxiously in the tunnel to take the field, he told them they had as many fans at the game as the Tigers did. They were skeptical, but then Vaught turned his team loose when he saw LSU running onto the field. Sure enough, the ovation was huge. "See, boys," he told his team in a huddle, "we have just as many fans here as they do."

It was the good old days.

It's a brutal truth that time just never stands still. The current of your life sweeps you along until you realize one day you've lived long enough to have a past. Part of it you cling to fondly. The stunts you pulled with your high-school buddies. Your first apartment. That dance with your first love. That special vacation. Those "good old days."

You hold on relentlessly to the memory of those old, familiar ways because of the stability they provide in our uncertain world. They will always be there even as times change and you age.

Another constant exists in your life, too. God has been a part of every event in your life that created a memory because he was there. He's always there with you; the question is whether you ignore him or make him a part of your day.

A "good old day" is any day shared with God.

We played in a golden era of football, when players held the sport and team performance in high regard.
--LSU All-American running back Jerry Stovall (1959-62)

Today is one of the "good old days"
if you share it with God.

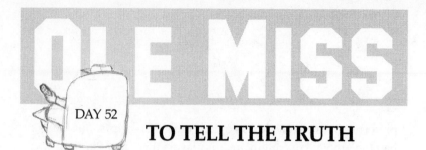

DAY 52

TO TELL THE TRUTH

Read Matthew 5:33-37.

"Simply let your 'Yes' be 'Yes,' and your 'No,' 'No';
anything beyond this comes from the evil one" (v. 37).

If the other team doesn't score, you can't lose." So spoke Ole Miss head coach David Cutcliffe, uttering one of football's great truths that the 2003 Egg Bowl had just illustrated.

An unrelenting rain for the Nov. 27 game didn't seem to bother the Rebels at all. Behind a defense that clearly wanted the series' first shutout of the Bulldogs since 1971, Ole Miss cruised to a 31-0 win. "Our defense played as good as it could play," declared Cutcliffe in laying down another truth that evening in Starkville.

The defense dominated in leading the Rebels to a share of the SEC's Western Division title. Ole Miss led 24-0 at halftime, and State's six possessions of the half ended four times with punts, once on downs, and once on an interception by linebacker Rob Robertson. At the break, the Rebs had rolled up 268 yards while holding the Bulldogs to a paltry 59 yards.

The ferocious Ole Miss defense generally harassed and frustrated the State quarterback all afternoon. The Dog signal caller was sacked three times, was intercepted once, and was hurried into making several throws that missed intended receivers.

Rebel defensive coordinator Chuck Driesbach joined Cutcliffe in praising the defense, saying, "I'd have to check the tape, but I think our defense maybe played its best game of the season."

REBELS

The defense clearly wanted the goose egg on the scoreboard. With nine minutes left to play and the Rebs up by 31, State was desperately trying to avoid the shutout with the ball at the Ole Miss 9. When a fourth-down pass play went awry, the defenders launched into a celebration.

The zero was labeled "one final exclamation point on a season of abject misery" for Mississippi State. It was also a reminder of the utter truth that if a team doesn't score, it can't win.

No, that dress doesn't make you look fat. But, officer, I wasn't speeding. I didn't get the project finished because I've been at the hospital every night with my ailing grandmother. What good-looking guy? I didn't notice.

Sometimes we lie to spare the feelings of others; more often, though, we lie to bail ourselves out of a jam, to make ourselves look better to others, or to gain the upper hand over someone.

But Jesus admonishes us to tell the truth. Frequently in our faith life we fret about what is right and what is wrong, but we can have no such ambivalence when it comes to telling the truth or lying. God and his son are so closely associated with the truth that lying is ultimately attributed to the devil ("the evil one"). Given his character, God cannot lie; given his character, the devil lies as a way of life. Given your character, which is it?

Trampling on the truth has become as commonplace as overpaid athletes and bad television.

-- Hockey coach Dan Bauer

**Jesus declared himself to be the truth,
so whose side are we on when we lie?**

A GENTLE MAN

Read John 2:13-22.

"He made a whip out of cords, and drove all from the temple area . . .; he scattered the coins of the money changers and overturned their tables" (v. 15).

A true Ole Miss legend was such a gentleman on the field that he warned a player before he retaliated for being held and also congratulated an opposing player after he threw a touchdown.

Almost forty years after he played his last down for the Rebels, Frank "Bruiser" Kinard was referred to as "perhaps the greatest tackle in football history." He lettered for three seasons (1935-37) and was a two-time All-America, the Rebels' first. He is a member of virtually every football hall of fame for which he is eligible.

Playing both ways at tackle, Kinard was so durable that his head coach, Ed Walker, claimed "he'll never get hurt" and didn't train a sub. He never needed one.

Kinard was also a true Southern gentleman, even on the field. In a service football game during World War II, he was consistently being held until he finally and matter-of-factly told the perpetrator, "Look. I'm small and I don't like to be held." That gentlemanly declaration didn't draw the desired response. A few plays later, the player left the game, rubbing and holding a bruised arm. He didn't return to action.

During a service game against a team of Marines, Kinard resented the team's intentionally roughing up a young black player.

He called them together and calmly warned them that if they didn't stop it, "You're going to hear from me." They backed off.

In the loss to State in 1936, an injured starter came in for the Dogs late in the game and threw a touchdown pass. Kinard went over to him and shook his hand, though the game wasn't over. He explained he had played high-school ball with the player and was glad he got to play. "I don't regret it," the gentleman said.

A calm, caring manner and a soft voice are often mistaken for weakness, and gentle men are frequently misunderstood by those who fail to appreciate their inner strength. But Frank Kinard's athletic career and Jesus' rampage through the Jerusalem temple illustrate the perils of underestimating a determined gentleman.

A gentleman treats other people kindly, respectfully, and justly, and conducts himself ethically in all situations. A gentleman doesn't lack resolve or backbone. Instead, he determines to live in a way that is exceedingly difficult in our selfish, me-first society; he lives the lifestyle God desires for us all.

Included in that mode of living is the understanding that the best way to have a request honored is to make it civilly, with a smile. God works that way too. He could bully you and boss you around; you couldn't stop him. But instead, he gently requests your attention and politely waits for the courtesy of a reply.

Play to win, observe the rules, and act like a gentleman.
-- Legendary basketball coach and author Clair Bee

God is a gentleman, soliciting your attention
politely and then patiently waiting for you
to give him the courtesy of a reply.

BEAUTIFUL PEOPLE

Read Matthew 23:23-28.

"Woe to you, teachers of the law and Pharisees, you hypocrites! You are like whitewashed tombs, which look beautiful on the outside, but on the inside are full of dead men's bones and everything unclean" (v. 27).

The Ole Miss freshman football team of 1967 had some special incentive to beat Mississippi State: They wanted to keep their good looks.

Freshman quarterback Archie Manning dubbed his first fall in Oxford the "Fall of Survival." "All of us lost weight," he recalled. "We had to write our weight down on a chart after every practice, and I remember writing '162' many a time, knowing I wasn't more than 156."

The Fall of Survival didn't start well for the freshman; they lost the opener to LSU. It got better after that, though, starting with a 21-2 whipping of Alabama. Skip Jernigan, who would become an All-SEC guard, recalled watching the Alabama players leave the field after the game "and coach Bear Bryant standing above them in the stands just glaring down at them. He was furious."

An undefeated Vanderbilt squad was bragging about its great freshman team. The Ole Miss coaches turned Manning loose on them, and the Rebel freshmen led 35-8 at halftime and won 80-8.

The season finale was against State. In those days, when the freshman arrived, the older guys would give them intentionally atrocious haircuts. Then shortly before the season started, they would shave the young players' heads. By the State game, the hair had grown back enough, as Manning recalled, "to maybe give a guy enough confidence to ask somebody for a date."

The varsity guys threatened the freshman with a new round of shaved heads if they lost to State. Thus inspired, the Ole Miss freshman rolled 49-7.

Remember the brunette who sat behind you in history class? Or the blonde in English? And how about that hunk from the next apartment who washes his car every Saturday morning and just forces you to get outside earlier than you really want to?

We do love those beautiful people.

It is worth remembering amid our adulation of and quest for superficial beauty that popular magazines such as *Vogue* or *People* probably wouldn't have been too enamored of Jesus' looks. Isaiah 53 declares that our savior "had no beauty or majesty to attract us to him, nothing in his appearance that we should desire him."

Though Jesus never urged folks to walk around with body odor and unwashed hair, he did admonish us to avoid being overly concerned with physical beauty, which fades with age despite tucks and Botox. What matters to God is inner beauty, which reveals itself in the practice of justice, mercy, and faith, and which is not only lifelong but eternal.

No way we were losing that game.
-- Archie Manning on the hairy incentive to beat State

When it comes to looking good to God,
it's what's inside that counts.

DAY 55

WORK ETHIC

Read Matthew 9:35-38.

"Then he said to his disciples, 'The harvest is plentiful but the workers are few. Ask the Lord of the harvest, therefore, to send out workers into his harvest field'" (vv. 37-38).

For Ole Miss volleyball star Regina Thomas, work is such a part of her character that she sings about it.

Rebel volleyball coach Joe Getzin first scouted Thomas in the spring of 2006 when she was a junior in high school. She was so good that even though she was hampered by a pulled muscle, Getzin was impressed. "She definitely caught my eye with her athleticism," the coach said.

Flash forward to the winter of 2011, and now Thomas is so good that she was named the program's first All-America (after 35 seasons) though a torn ACL ended her season prematurely and kept her out of the NCAA Tournament. A middle blocker, Thomas was also named first-team All-SEC in 2011 after posting the highest hitting percentage the league has seen in the last seven seasons and the fourth best percentage in the country.

Regina Thomas is really good. But there's more.

All those years ago when Getzin first saw Thomas play, he was impressed not only with her athleticism but her attitude. Even then, she was the kind "of a kid that would do anything to win," the coach said. Especially if that "anything" involves work.

Thomas' work ethic so took over the mentality of the Ole Miss volleyball team that she and her teammates even sang about work while they were playing. "Work, work, all day long" went the lyrics, and everyone on the team knew the tune. Thomas said the song reflected how hard the players who man the middle positions work in practice. "We're weird, we know, but we work hard," she said, "so we feel we deserve our own theme song."

In Regina Thomas' case, the combination of awesome talent and a work ethic so ingrained she sings about it resulted in an All-American career.

Do you embrace hard work or try to avoid it? No matter how hard you may try, you really can't escape hard work. Funny thing about all these labor-saving devices like cell phones and laptop computers: You're working longer and harder than ever.

For many of us, our work defines us more than any other aspect of our lives. But there's a workforce you're a part of that doesn't show up in any Labor Department statistics or any IRS records.

You're part of God's staff; God has a specific job that only you can do for him. It's often referred to as a "calling," but it amounts to your serving God where there is a need in the way that best suits your God-given abilities and talents

You should stand ready to work for God all the time, 24-7. Those are awful hours, but the benefits are out of this world.

We are just really hard workers.
                    — Regina Thomas on the players in the middle

**God calls you to work for him using the talents
and gifts he gave you; whether you're a worker
or a malingerer is up to you.**

DAY 56

HOMELESS

Read Matthew 8:18-22.

"Jesus replied, 'Foxes have holes and birds of the air have nests, but the Son of Man has no place to lay his head'" (v. 20).

In 1913, the Ole Miss football team hit the road for one of the most bizarre schedules in football history.

From 1912-24, Ole Miss had seven head football coaches in an ongoing search for stability. "It was a time," said Jeff Hamm, a student from 1913-17 who went on to serve the university for forty years in various capacities, "when I had doors slammed in my face if I brought up support for football."

With limited support and limited funds, the football team was in effect homeless, playing most of its games on the road. The 1914 team, for instance, played only two of its ten games in Oxford. No road warriors in Ole Miss history, however, can come up with anything to match what the team of 1913 (which had only two home games) did at the beginning of its season and at the end.

The season opened with a road trip to Virginia that had the team play three games in eight days. The Rebs lost to VMI 14-0 on Oct. 8 and to VPI 35-14 three days later. They then took on Virginia Medical four days later. Frank Smythe caught a touchdown pass from fullback Harley Harris, and the defense made the lone score stand up for a 7-6 win.

That was strange enough. But on Nov. 27, the Rebs ended the

season by playing two games at locations 384 miles apart.

Head coach Bill Driver decided to take his first team to Arkadelphia, Ark., for a game against Ouachita Baptist. He put his second team under the leadership of team captain Forrest McCall and sent them to Hattiesburg for a game against Mississippi Normal College (Southern Miss). All in all, the strangest road trip in school history didn't turn out too badly. Ole Miss beat Normal 13-7 and tied the Baptists 0-0.

Rock bottom in America has a face: the bag lady pushing a shopping cart; the scruffy guy with a beard and a backpack at the interstate exit holding a cardboard sign. Look closer at that bag lady or that scruffy guy, though, and you may see desperate women with children fleeing violence, veterans haunted by their combat experiences, or sick or injured workers.

Few of us are indifferent to the homeless when we're around them. They often raise quite strong passions, whether we regard them as a ministry or an odorous nuisance. They trouble us, perhaps because we realize that we're only one catastrophic illness and a few paychecks away from joining them. They remind us of how tenuous our own holds upon material success really are.

But they also stir our compassion because we serve a Lord who – like them -- had no home, and for whom, the homeless, too, are his children.

Some people beat up on the homeless for sport.
-- Maryland State Sen. Lisa Gladden

**Because they, too, are God's children,
the homeless merit our compassion, not our scorn.**

CELEBRATION TIME

Read Luke 15:1-10.

"There is rejoicing in the presence of the angels of God over one sinner who repents" (v. 10).

On Sept. 27, 2008, the Rebs played better than they celebrated.

On that legendary day, Ole Miss stunned 4th-ranked Florida 31-30, an upset that left Heisman-Trophy winner Tim Tebow in tears and that caught the attention of the nation. "We can build on this," said Ole Miss head coach Houston Nutt about the importance of the win.

Sophomore quarterback Jevan Snead threw two touchdown passes and ran for another score in leading the Rebels to the win. While he was only 9-of-20 passing for 185 yards, he made the big plays when Ole Miss needed them.

Snead's biggest play of the game was his 86-yard throw-and-catch touchdown with Shay Hodge. That came with 5:26 to play and put the Rebs up 31-24. But sophomore defensive end Kentrell Lockett had a play just as big when the Gators rallied for a touchdown. He sailed across the line and blocked the conversion try that was the difference in the game. "When I crossed the line, I made up my mind I was going to get the block," he said.

The Rebel defense, which finished the season as the fourth-best in the country against the rush, stopped Tebow on fourth and two feet at the Ole Miss 32 with about 40 seconds to play. From there, Snead took a couple of knees and the celebration began.

REBELS

Some of it the Rebs handled just fine. They cavorted with the band and were raucous in the locker room. Their handling of the Gatorade bucket, however, needed some work. During the dousing of the coach that is now a routine and necessary part of the celebration of big wins, they hit Nutt with the bucket instead of the Gatorade, leaving him with a bloody nose.

Ole Miss just whipped State. You got that new job or that promotion. You just held your newborn child in your arms. Life has those grand moments that call for celebration. You may jump up and down and scream in a wild frenzy or share a quiet, sedate candlelight dinner at home -- but you celebrate.

Consider then a celebration that is beyond our imagining, one that fills every niche and corner of the very home of God and the angels. Imagine a celebration in Heaven, which also has its grand moments.

Those grand moments are touched off when someone comes to faith in Jesus. Heaven itself rings with the joyous sounds of the singing and dancing of the celebrating angels. Even God rejoices when just one person – you or someone you have introduced to Christ? -- turns to him.

When you said "yes" to Christ, you made the angels dance.

They've got to get better at [celebrating wins]. I hope they get a lot of practice.
-- A bloodied Houston Nutt after the Florida win

God himself joins the angels in heavenly celebration when even a single person turns to him through faith in Jesus.

HOW DISAPPOINTING

Read Ezra 3.

"Many of the older priests and Levites and family heads, who had seen the former temple, wept aloud when they saw the foundation of this temple being laid, while many others shouted for joy" (v. 12).

The Ole Miss players were once so disappointed with their up-coming bowl trip that they threatened a boycott of the game over a suit of clothes.

The 1947 Rebels, Johnny Vaught's first team, went 8-2 and won the SEC title for the first time. Quarterback Charley Conerly and end Barney Poole were both All-America; Buddy Bowen won the Jacobs Blocking Trophy as the SEC's best blocker; tackle Bill Erickson was second-team All-SEC. Conerly set an NCAA record for completions in a season and finished fourth in the balloting for the Heisman Trophy. Poole's total of fifty-two catches was a new NCAA record. Vaught was named the SEC Coach of the Year.

It was the biggest season in Ole Miss football history. The Rebs were obviously strong enough to have several bowls, including the Sugar and the Orange, courting them. But in a rather strange circumstance, in June before the season even began, officials from the Delta Bowl in Memphis extended an invitation to the Rebels to play in their inaugural game. They guaranteed the team $25,000; a program that needed money and had gone 2-7 the season before couldn't count on a better offer. The Rebs accepted.

REBELS

So the players watched lesser SEC teams land the more glamorous bowls. Their disappointment grew when the suit of clothes they had been promised by bowl officials didn't arrive. Several players telegraphed the sponsors, threatening a boycott if they didn't get their suits. Vaught intervened and ended that notion.

Disappointed or not, the Rebels played and won, beating TCU, Vaught's alma mater, 13-9 on an icy New Year's Day in Memphis.

We know disappointment. Friends lie to us or betray us; we lose our jobs through no fault of our own; distance grows between us and our children; the Rebels lose; our dreams shatter.

Disappointment occurs when something or somebody fails to meet our expectations, which inevitably will happen. Crucial to our life, therefore, is handling disappointment rather than uselessly trying to avoid it.

The reaction of the old people of Israel at the dedication of the temple is not a good example for us. Instead of joyously celebrating the construction of a new place of worship, they bemoaned the lost glories of the old one. They chose disappointment over a long-gone past rather than the wonders of the present reality.

Disappointment can paralyze us all, but only if we lose sight of an immutable truth: Our lives may not always be what we wish they were, but God is still good to us.

There's nothing disappointing about that.

We might as well win.
-- Charley Conerly on playing in the Delta Bowl

**Even in disappointing times, we can be confident
that God is with us and therefore life is good.**

SMART MOVE

Read 1 Kings 4:29-34; 11:1-6.

"[Solomon] was wiser than any other man. . . . As Solomon grew old, his wives turned his heart after other gods, and his heart was not fully devoted to the Lord his God" (vv. 4:31, 11:4).

Sean Tuohy made a smart move when he decided to play basketball for Ole Miss. Playing time played a part in that carefully considered decision. But so did the girls.

Tuohy is probably most famous now for *The Blind Side*, but anyone familiar with Ole Miss basketball knows his place in the program's history. He was honored as an SEC Legend in 2006; in 1998, he was inducted into the Mississippi Athletic Hall of Fame. From 1979-82, Tuohy handed out 830 assists, which still stands as the SEC career record. His 260 assists in 1980 remains the league single-season record. He was All-SEC three times and was captain of the 1981 team that won the SEC Tournament.

Tuohy grew up in New Orleans as LSU basketball was gathering steam under Dale Brown. So why did he decide to leave his home state and make what was ultimately a really smart move?

Basically, Tuohy had four reasons. "Ole Miss was just horrible," he admitted. That was reason number one: He would get to play right away and would play a lot, whereas LSU had Ethan Martin, which was reason number two. "I wasn't stupid enough to think I was going to beat him out."

REBELS

Tuohy wanted to stay in the SEC, which was reason number three: "I wanted to be on TV on the SEC Game of the Week."

Then there was reason number four: girls. "Ole Miss had 1.2 girls to every guy student," he said. "If everyone has to have a date, on sheer numbers alone, I'm in. I needed the numbers."

With those carefully considered reasons, Sean Tuohy made the smart move and became the consummate point guard.

Remember that time you wrecked the car when you spilled hot coffee on your lap? That cold morning you fell out of the boat? The time you gave your honey a tool box for her birthday?

Formal education notwithstanding, we all make some dumb moves sometimes because time spent in a classroom is not an accurate gauge of common sense. Folks impressed with their own smarts often grace us with erudite pronouncements that we intuitively recognize as flawed, unworkable, or simply wrong.

A good example is the observation that great intelligence and scholarship are inherently incompatible with a deep and abiding faith in God. That is, the more we know, the less we believe. Any incompatibility occurs, however, only because we begin to trust in our own wisdom rather than the wisdom of God. We forget, as Solomon did, that God is the ultimate source of all our knowledge and wisdom and that even our ability to learn is a gift from God.

Not smart at all.

When I got [to Ole Miss], I knew what would keep me on the bench and what would put me on the court and keep me there.
-- Sean Tuohy on his smart move to help others score

Being truly smart means trusting in God's wisdom rather than only in our own knowledge.

AMAZING!

Read: Luke 4:31-36.

"All the people were amazed and said to each other, 'What is this teaching? With authority and power he gives orders to evil spirits and they come out!'" (v. 36

What the Ole Miss defense did in the 1992 Egg Bowl was nothing short of amazing.

It was dubbed "The Stand," and it enabled the Rebels to escape with a 17-10 win in one of the most ferocious games in the rivalry's long history. Both teams were 7-3 and bowl-bound. (The Rebels would whip Air Force 13-0 in the Liberty Bowl.)

The Dogs scored all ten of their points within a three-minute span of the second quarter. Ole Miss answered when quarterback Russ Shows threw a 7-yard TD pass to fullback Marvin Courtney. In the third quarter, Cory Philpot's 7-yard run gave the Rebels their first lead. Brian Lee's 22-yard field goal with 10:50 left in the game made it 17-10.

From there, the Ole Miss defense took over.

Two possessions later, the Dogs sat at the Rebel 8. First play: 2-yard gain up the middle. Play No. 2: Chad Brown and Cassius Ware dropped the runner for a 4-yard loss. 2:35 left to play. No. 3: Michael Lowery intercepted a pass and was downed at the 3.

Two plays later, the Rebs fumbled at the 8. Nos. 4 and 5: incomplete passes. No. 6: 3-yard loss. No. 7: incomplete pass but an interference call set the ball at the 2 and gave State a first down.

REBELS

Play No. 8: 1-yard gain. No. 9: 3-yard loss. Only 47 seconds left to play and State called a time out. No. 10: 2-yard loss. Fourth down with 24 seconds left. Play No. 11: incomplete pass into the end zone with the quarterback throwing under pressure.

Amazed by what they had witnessed, Ole Miss fans assaulted the goalposts. The defense had made an 11-play goal-line stand.

The word *amazing* defines the limits of what you believe to be plausible or usual. The Grand Canyon, the birth of your children, those last-second Ole Miss wins and goal-line stands -- they're amazing! You've never seen anything like that before!

Some people in Galilee felt the same way when they encountered Jesus. Jesus amazed them with the authority of his teaching, and he wowed them with his power over spirit beings. People everywhere just couldn't quit talking about him.

It would have been amazing had they not been amazed. They were, after all, witnesses to the most amazing spectacle in the history of the world: God himself was right there among them walking, talking, teaching, preaching, and healing.

Their amazement should also be a part of your life because Jesus still lives. The almighty and omnipotent God of the universe seeks to spend time with you every day – because he loves you. Amazing!

I've never seen an effort like that by the guys in red shirts.
-- Head coach Billy Brewer on the goal-line stand

Everything about God is amazing,
but perhaps most amazing of all is that
he loves us and desires our company.

MAKE NO MISTAKE

Read Mark 14:66-72.

*"Then Peter remembered the word Jesus had spoken to
him: 'Before the rooster crows twice you will disown me
three times.' And he broke down and wept" (v. 72).*

One newspaper called it "The Goof That Laid the Golden Egg."
Nevertheless, the mistake was crucial in the Rebels' drive to yet
another SEC and national championship.

The 1962 team remains the only one in Ole Miss football history to complete the season unbeaten and untied. The squad won
the program's fifth SEC title and its third national championship. Quarterback Glynn Griffing and tackle Jim Dunaway were
All-Americas. The defense led the nation by allowing only 142.2
yards per game.

With everything on the line, the Rebs ran into some surprising
resistance from a 3-5 Mississippi State team in the Egg Bowl in
Oxford. The Bulldogs jumped out to a 6-0 lead when they drove
66 yards on their first possession. They couldn't do anything with
the Rebel defense after that, but they refused to fold.

In the second quarter, Ole Miss drove 82 yards, halfback
Louis Guy scoring from the one and Billy Carl Irwin kicking the
extra point. The score stayed at 7-6 until late in the game when
quarterback Jim Weatherly faked a handoff to halfback Dave Jennings and bootlegged around the right side for a 43-yard TD run
that put the final of 13-6 on the scoreboard.

REBELS

The play obviously surprised the State defense, but it came as a surprise to the Rebels too. In the huddle, they had called a simple handoff to Jennings, who would hit the middle. The truth came out after the game: The touchdown had come on a botched play. Weatherly had failed to get the ball to Jennings and then had stuck the ball on his hip and headed wide to see what he could get.

It's distressing but it's true: Like Ole Miss football teams and like Simon Peter, we all make mistakes. Only one perfect man ever walked on this earth, and no one of us is he. Some mistakes are just dumb. Like locking yourself out of your car or falling into a swimming pool with your clothes on.

Other mistakes are more significant. Like heading down a path to addiction. Committing a crime. Walking out on a spouse and the children.

All these mistakes, however, from the momentarily annoying to the life-altering tragic, share one aspect: They can all be forgiven in Christ. Other folks may not forgive us; we may not even forgive ourselves. But God will forgive us when we call upon him in Jesus' name.

Thus, the twofold fatal mistake we can make is ignoring the fact that we will die one day and subsequently ignoring the fact that Jesus is the only way to shun Hell and enter Heaven. We absolutely must get this one right.

I missed the handoff.
-- Jim Weatherly on the goof that laid the golden egg

**Only one mistake we make sends us to Hell
when we die: ignoring Jesus while we live.**

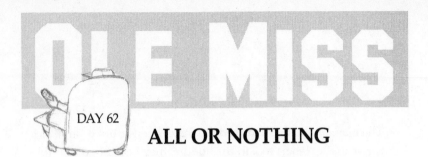

DAY 62

ALL OR NOTHING

Read Deuteronomy 6:4-9.

"Love the Lord your God with all your heart and with all your soul and with all your strength" (v. 5).

Ole Miss needed him, and Johnny Vaught loved the school too much to refuse.

Heart problems forced the legendary head coach to step down after the 1970 season. (See Devotion No. 100.) His successor, Billy Kinard, got off to a flying start with a 10-2 record in 1971. But a 5-5 record in 1972 amounted to what one writer called an "obituary" since it snapped Ole Miss' successive string of bowl appearances at fifteen. Alumni were grumbling, and early in 1973, reports of dissension on the team surfaced.

After a 17-13 loss to Memphis State that left the Rebels 1-2, the powers-that-be decided a change had to be made. The chancellor and the head of the athletic committee met and decided only the legend could heal the breach and settle things down.

Vaught rejected their overture. "I am not interested," he said. "I don't think I ought to get back in." Word of the effort to lure Vaught out of retirement quickly made its way to the students, and chants of "We want Vaught" reverberated across campus.

A delegation approached Vaught again, and a meeting at the coach's home ended when he said, "Gentlemen, I love Ole Miss. I would do anything for it once." Johnny Vaught was back.

Only hours later he met with what was now his team and immediately let them know why he had come back. "Gentlemen, we are in a situation that I didn't ask for, but I love Ole Miss and let's go out and make the best of it," he said.

The love was reciprocal. The following Saturday, when Ole Miss threw an incomplete long pass on its first play, the team received a standing ovation.

Unlike Johnny Vaught, whose love for Ole Miss was deep and true, all too many sports fans cheer when their team is winning championships, but they're the first to criticize or turn silent when losses and disappointments come. They're fair-weather fans.

The true fans stick with the Rebels no matter what, which is exactly the way God commands us to love him. Sure, this mandate is eons old, but the principle it established in our relationship with God has not changed. If anything, it has gained even more immediacy in our materialistic, secular culture that demands we love and worship anything and anybody but God.

Moreover, since God gave the original command, he has sent us Jesus. Thus, we today are even more indebted to God's grace and have even more reason to love God than did the Israelites to whom the original command was given.

God gave us everything; in return, we are to love him with everything we have and everything we are.

It was like Santa Claus had been to see you. When he got through talking, everybody stood up and cheered and there were a lot of wet eyes.
-- Senior Harry Harrison on Johnny Vaught's return

With all we have and all we are –
that's the way we are to love God.

DAY 63

THE FAME GAME

Read 1 Kings 10:1-10, 18-29.

"King Solomon was greater in riches and wisdom than all the other kings of the earth. The whole world sought audience with Solomon" (vv. 23-24).

Ole Miss senior guard Bianca Thomas just wasn't very famous -- until the night she lit LSU up for 42.

Even after Thomas was named first-team All-SEC as a junior in 2009, she still must have suffered from a lack of name recognition. That's the only way to explain the rather strange fact that she was a preseason pick in 2010 for the All-SEC *second* team.

One writer noted that prior to that now-legendary LSU game, the only people who really knew how good Thomas was were her teammates and coaches and the WNBA scouts. That all changed on the night of Jan. 17, 2010, when Thomas became only the fifteenth player in NCAA women's basketball history to score 40-or-more points in a game. She poured in 42, a Tad Smith Coliseum record, as the Rebels upset No. 12 LSU 80-71. "I've never seen anything quite like that," commented teammate Shantell Black.

No matter what the Tigers did, it didn't matter. They were physical, trying to deny her the ball. They stalked her. They switched off. They double-teamed. And Thomas hit shot after shot.

So why wasn't she more famous before the LSU game? "She's always been quiet," explained assistant coach Armintie Price. "But now she's letting her game speak for her and people are finding out that it's speaking very loudly."

Thomas finished her senior season as quite the celebrity. She led the SEC in scoring, was first-team All-SEC again, and was taken in the first round of the WNBA draft.

Have you ever wanted to be famous? Hanging out with other rich and famous people, having folks with microphones listen to what you say, throwing money around like toilet paper, meeting adoring and clamoring fans, signing autographs, and posing for the paparazzi before you climb into your imported sports car?

Many of us yearn to be famous, well-known in the places and by the people that we believe matter. That's all fame amounts to: strangers knowing your name and your face.

The truth is that you are already famous where it really does matter, which excludes TV's talking heads, screaming teenagers, rapt moviegoers, or D.C. power brokers. You are famous because Almighty God knows your name, your face, and everything else there is to know about you.

If a persistent photographer snapped you pondering this fame – the only kind that has eternal significance – would the picture show the world unbridled joy or the shell-shocked expression of a mug shot?

I can't understand why people haven't been talking about her all season, but I think she has everyone's attention now.
– UM coach Renee Ladner on Bianca Thomas after the LSU game

**You're already famous because God
knows your name and your face,
which may be either reassuring or terrifying.**

DAY 64

NAME DROPPING

Read Exodus 3:13-20.

"God said to Moses, 'I AM WHO I AM. This is what you are to say to the Israelites: 'I AM has sent me to you'" *(v. 14).*

One of the most influential figures in the history of Ole Miss athletics also had one of its greatest nicknames.

Claude M. Smith was born in 1905 on a farm at Heucks Creek outside Brookhaven. He spent his early years "milking crows and playing with lightning bugs." When he was "a little bitty thing," he fell into a drainage ditch at the school house and came out covered with mud. A schoolmate took one look at him and said, "You look just like a tadpole." Tadpole Smith it would be.

Smith spent the summer of 1925 driving railroad spikes, but he saw little future in it. Instead, he wanted to go to college and play football and baseball. A Hattiesburg attorney drove him to Oxford and he never left.

From 1926-28, Smith combined exceptional speed with a sense of derring-do to earn a reputation as the greatest punt returner in the South. As a halfback, he played without a helmet and taped his ears back so nothing would slow him down. He also played first base for the Rebel baseball team that won the Southern Conference championship in 1929 when he was a senior.

Upon graduation, Tadpole joined coach Homer Hazel's staff. He coached the freshmen for twelve seasons and was the head baseball coach for fifteen seasons. When he came back to Oxford after World War II, he was named athletic director. During his tenure, "he brought the physical facilities out of the dark ages."

Both a state and university sports hall-of-famer, Smith retired in 1970. In 1972, Rebel Coliseum was renamed C.M. "Tad" Smith Coliseum, the only facility in the country named after a tadpole.

Nicknames such as Tadpole Smith are usually not slapped haphazardly upon individuals but rather reflect widely held perceptions about the person named. Proper names do that also.

Nowhere throughout history has this concept been more prevalent than in the Bible, where a name is not a mere label but is an expression of the essential nature of the named one. That is, a person's name reveals his or her character. Even God shares this concept; to know the name of God is to know God as he has chosen to reveal himself to us.

What does your name say about you? Honest, trustworthy, a seeker of the truth and a person of God? Or does the mention of your name cause your coworkers to whisper snide remarks, your neighbors to roll their eyes, or your friends to start making allowances for you?

Most importantly, what does your name say about you to God? He, too, knows you by name.

A good nickname inspires awe and ensures that you'll be enshrined in the Pantheon of [Sports] Legends.
                                                          -- Funny Sports Quotes blog

**Live so that your name evokes positive
associations by people you know,
by the public, and by God.**

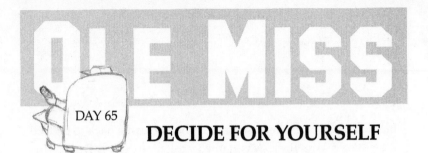

DECIDE FOR YOURSELF

Read John 6:60-69.

"The words I have spoken to you are spirit and they are life. Yet there are some of you who do not believe" (vv. 63b-64a).

Tommy Tuberville is widely known in his profession as something of a riverboat gambler. He certainly lived up to that reputation with a decision he made in the 1997 Egg Bowl.

To say that both teams were fired up about this latest renewal of college football's tenth longest uninterrupted series would be a real understatement seeing as how a fight broke out between the players during warmups. This less-than-gentlemanly disagreement required coaches, referees, and highway patrolmen to quell it. For the rest of the day, the teams had to enter and leave their dressing rooms at different times. In keeping with the spirit of the rivalry, each team blamed the other for starting the spat.

Once the game began, though, the fighting stopped and the playing began in a light rain. Ole Miss took the opening kickoff 71 yards for a touchdown. Part of the efficiency resulted from quarterback Stewart Patridge's daily exercise of throwing a wet ball some at practice. The score came on a 35-yard pass from Patridge to halfback Andre Rone. Steve Lindsey's kick made it 7-0.

That was pretty much it, though, for the Rebel offense until it got the ball with only 2:12 to play and State leading 14-7. Patridge used 1:47 to complete six of nine passes and lead the Rebs 64 yards for a score. With 25 seconds left, he hit Rone from ten yards out.

Now, the decision was Tuberville's to make. Go for the tie and overtime or go for the win now? The head coach knew that his team had been beaten up pretty well by the larger Bulldogs; their tanks were running low. He decided to go for the win. Wide receiver Cory Peterson ran a crossing route just beyond the goal line, and Patridge found him. "It was the biggest play of Stew's life and maybe all of our lives," Peterson said. Ole Miss had a 15-14 win.

As with Tommy Tuberville, the decisions you have made along the way have shaped your life at every pivotal moment. Some decisions you made suddenly and carelessly; some you made carefully and deliberately; some were forced upon you. You may have discovered that some of those spur-of-the-moment decisions have turned out better than your carefully considered ones.

Of all your life's decisions, however, none is more important than one you cannot ignore: What have you done with Jesus? Even in his time, people chose to follow Jesus or to reject him, and nothing has changed; the decision must still be made and nobody can make it for you. Ignoring Jesus won't work either; that is, in fact, a decision, and neither he nor the consequences of your decision will go away.

Carefully considered or spontaneous – how you arrive at a decision for Jesus doesn't matter; all that matters is that you get there.

I changed my mind twice, but went with my first instinct to go for two.
-- Tommy Tuberville on his decision to go for the win

A decision for Jesus may be spontaneous or
considered; what counts is that you make it.

FEAR FACTOR

Read Matthew 14:22-33.

"[The disciples] cried out in fear. But Jesus immediately said to them: 'Take courage! It is I. Don't be afraid'" (vv. 26-27).

Hall-of-Famer Charlie Flowers was afraid at least once in his legendary Ole Miss football career -- and he wasn't even on the field at the time.

From 1957-59, Flowers played fullback on three teams that were a combined 28-4-1 and won three bowl games. He was first-team All-America as a senior in '59 as he led the SEC in both scoring and rushing and finished fifth in the voting for the Heisman Trophy. He set a school record for career rushing yardage, and his average of 5.64 yards per carry in '59 was also a school record. Decades later, Flowers' magnificent season ranks behind only the 5.97 average set by Randy Baldwin. Flowers was inducted into the College Football Hall of Fame in 1997.

After an 8-2 season in 1958, the Rebels met the Florida Gators in the Gator Bowl. Ole Miss was a one-touchdown favorite until a pre-game storm turned the field into a mud wallow. Said one writer, it was "a dismal, drizmal day more fitten for beast than man." On the sludgy field, the Rebs pulled out a 7-3 win.

Junior quarterback Bobby Franklin was the game's MVP, but he sent Flowers to the sideline in the first quarter when he accidentally kicked his fullback in the head during a pileup. Team physician Ferrell Varner saw some blood above an eye and escorted the woozy Flowers into the dressing room.

After a few minutes, Flowers came around and heard cheering outside. His eyes then grew wide with alarm. He propped himself up on one elbow and announced, "Doc, I'm going to die." Varner said he wasn't but Flowers was not convinced. Finally, Varner asked, "Why, Charlie?" He answered, "Well, Ole Miss is out there playing football and you're in here with me."

Some fears are universal; others are particular. Speaking to the Rotary Club may require a heavy dose of antiperspirant. Elevator walls may feel as though they're closing in on you. And don't even get started on being in the dark with spiders and snakes during a thunderstorm.

We all live in fear, and God knows this. Dozens of passages in the Bible urge us not to be afraid. God isn't telling us to lose our wariness of oncoming cars or big dogs with nasty dispositions; this is a helpful fear God instilled in us for protection.

What God does wish driven from our lives is a spirit of fear that dominates us, that makes our lives miserable and keeps us from doing what we should, such as sharing our faith. In commanding that we not be afraid, God reminds us that when we trust completely in him, we find peace that calms our fears.

Let me win. But if I cannot win, let me be brave in the attempt.
— Special Olympics Motto

You have your own peculiar set of fears,
but they should never paralyze you
because God is greater than anything you fear.

MIRACLE PLAY

Read Matthew 12:38-42.

"He answered, 'A wicked and adulterous generation asks for a miraculous sign!'" (v. 39)

Even the Ole Miss head coach called the win "miraculous."

The Rebels opened the 1981 football season on Sept. 5 against Tulane in the Superdome. Ole Miss dominated the first half and led 12-0 at the break but had a touchdown nullified on the last play of the half. "I've never seen anything take so much out of a team as that took out of ours," head coach Steve Sloan said.

The result was Tulane domination in the last half and an 18-12 lead as the game wore down. With only 2:13 left, the Rebels were in a whole lot of trouble. They had the ball, but at their own 4. And they were without All-SEC quarterback John Fourcade, sidelined with a shoulder injury. Soph Kelly Powell was at the helm.

"All seemed so very hopeless for Ole Miss." It would obviously take a miracle for the Rebs to pull out a win.

Two completions to tailback Buford McGee carried to the 45. A strike to tight end Steve Deane gained seven more yards before wide receiver Breck Tyler's catch moved the ball to the Wave 39.

Then came the miracle. With just over a minute left, the Rebels called for a simple curl pattern with Powell once again looking for Tyler. But as the play unfolded, Powell saw a lot of open field. He pointed Tyler toward the end zone. "I didn't know what I was doing," Tyler said, "but I headed that way. It was probably the

REBELS

worst pattern I've ever run."

Maybe, but he made one of his best catches ever, snatching Powell's pass away from a Tulane cornerback and falling into the end zone to complete a 96-yard drive. Todd Gatlin kicked the extra point with 1:01 left for a 19-18 Rebel lead. When Freddie Joe Nunn blocked a long Tulane field goal, the miracle was complete.

Miracles defy rational explanation – like a late touchdown drive that pulls off a miraculous comeback. Or escaping with minor abrasions from an accident that totals your car. Or recovering from an illness that seemed terminal. Underlying the notion of miracles is the idea that they are rare instances of direct divine intervention that reveal God.

But life shows us quite the contrary, that miracles are anything but rare. Since God made the world and everything in it, everything around you is miraculous. Even you are a miracle. Your life thus can be mundane, dull, and ordinary, or it can be spent in a glorious attitude of childlike wonder and awe. It depends on whether or not you see the world through the eyes of faith. Only through faith can you discern the hand of God in any event; only through faith can you see the miraculous and thus see God.

Jesus knew that miracles don't produce faith, but rather faith produces miracles.

Do you believe in miracles? Yes!
– Al Michaels when U.S. defeated USSR in hockey in 1980
Winter Games

Miracles are all around us,
but it takes the eyes of faith to see them.

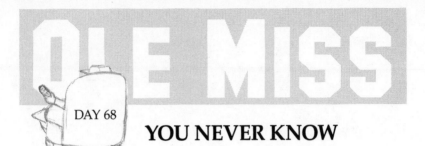

YOU NEVER KNOW

Read Exodus 3:1-12.

"But Moses said to God, 'Who am I, that I should go to Pharaoh and bring the Israelites out of Egypt?' And God said, 'I will be with you'" (vv. 11-12a).

Eli Manning didn't have Ole Miss on his short list. Ole Miss wasn't even recruiting him hard. But then something happened.

The younger Manning, of course, played quarterback for the Rebels from 2000-03, setting or tying 45 game, season, and career records. His senior season he was the SEC Player of the Year and won the Maxwell Award as the nation's best all-around player and the Johnny Unitas Golden Arm Award as the country's top quarterback. He finished third in the Heisman voting.

Eli's lineage is so well known as to bar any worthwhile discussion. As he considered where to play college football, "comparisons with his father [didn't] bother Eli." Brother Peyton's legacy did, however. "It would have been too much to deal with," he said, which explains why he told David Cutcliffe, Tennessee's offensive coordinator, that he would not be coming to Knoxville.

So that made Ole Miss the logical choice? Not at all.

At the time, Manning had narrowed his choices down to Texas and Virginia. Part of his disinterest in Oxford lay in the school's disinterest toward him. Rebel head coach Tommy Tuberville was looking elsewhere for his quarterback of the future. Archie Manning said, "I sensed that it really bothered Eli that Ole Miss wasn't recruiting him harder."

But you never know. Two weeks after Eli had talked to Cutcliffe, the coach called him back with news that changed everything: He had been named the new head coach at Ole Miss. One of the new coach's first priorities was a visit to the Manning home.

The rest, of course, is glorious Ole Miss gridiron history.

You never know how things will turn out in life, just as you never know what you can do until you want to bad enough or until – like Moses -- you have to. Serving in the military, maybe even in combat. Standing by a friend while everyone else unjustly excoriates her. Playing football at a school where you father's legacy is everywhere. Undergoing agonizing medical treatment and managing to smile. You never know where life will take you or what it will demand of you.

It's that way too in your relationship with God. As Moses discovered, you never know where or when God will call you or what God will ask of you. You do know that God expects you to be faithful and willing to trust him even when he calls you to tasks that daunt and dismay you.

You can respond faithfully to whatever it is God calls you to do. That's because even though you never know what lies ahead, you do know that God will lead you and will provide what you need.

There's one word to describe baseball: You never know.

– Yogi Berra

**You never know what God will ask you to do,
but you always know he will provide
everything you need to do it.**

DAY 69

FAMILY TIES

Read Mark 3:31-35.

"[Jesus] said, 'Here are my mother and my brothers! Whoever does God's will is my brother and sister and mother'" (vv. 34-35).

His family kept a future All-America from playing football for LSU instead of Ole Miss.

Glynn Griffing was first-team All-America in 1962 when, as a senior, he quarterbacked the Rebels to an undefeated season and their second national championship in three seasons. He was inducted into the Ole Miss Hall of Fame in 1989 and the Mississippi Sports Hall of Fame in 2002.

Griffing was "the first graduate of little Culkin High School to win a major college scholarship." The problem facing Ole Miss in its recruitment of Griffing was that Culkin is closer to Baton Rouge than it is to Oxford. "I really wanted to go to LSU at first," Griffing said.

LSU head coach Paul Dietzel wanted Griffing. He appeared to cinch the deal when he showed up at the Griffing household one morning before breakfast. "Mother fixed him bacon and eggs and he certainly impressed me," Griffing recalled. As he left, Dietzel told his recruit, "Glynn, I've got a bunk at LSU with your name on it." Griffing replied, "I'll be there."

When he returned home late that afternoon after school, Griffing was still excited about the decision he had made. The rest of

REBELS

the household wasn't, though. His parents weren't convinced at all that he should play for the Tigers. "If you are going to live in Mississippi, you ought to go to school in Mississippi," the senior Griffing told his son.

His family's lack of enthusiasm for LSU "turned my thinking around," said Griffing. He visited Ole Miss and was impressed. When he announced he was headed to Oxford, his family was with him this time.

Some wit said families are like fudge, mostly sweet with a few nuts. You can probably call the names of your sweetest relatives, whom you cherish, and of the nutty ones too, whom you mostly try to avoid at a family reunion.

Like it or not, you have a family, and that's God's doing. God cherishes the family so much that he chose to live in one as a son, a brother, and a cousin.

One of Jesus' more startling actions was to redefine the family. No longer is it a single household of blood relatives or even a clan or a tribe. Jesus' family is the result not of an accident of birth but rather a conscious choice. All those who do God's will are members of Jesus' family.

What a startling and downright wonderful thought! You have family members out there you don't even know who stand ready to love you just because you're part of God's family.

Chalk one up for our family affair.
-- Johnny Vaught on landing Glynn Griffing

**For followers of Jesus, family comes not from
a shared ancestry but from a shared faith.**

IN THE KNOW

Read John 4:19-26, 39-42.

"They said to the woman, . . . 'Now we have heard for ourselves, and we know that this man really is the Savior of the world'" (v. 42).

Rolling to an 8-0-2 season, the Rebels of 1952 pulled off what was called "the most significant victory ever recorded" by the school. They managed it largely because they knew something.

Starting slowly, the team was only 2-0-2 and had managed a tie with Vanderbilt only because junior guard Crawford Mims blocked a punt out of the end zone for a safety. A disgruntled coach Johnny Vaught called in his seniors for a less-than-warm-and-fuzzy get-together. In turn, they delivered the message to the rest of the team. The result was four straight wins.

The whole time, though, all eyes were on the ninth game of the season, a date with mighty Maryland. The Terrapins came to town ranked No. 3 and riding a 22-game unbeaten streak, the longest in the country.

Vaught began preparing for the Maryland game even before the season began. In August, he commissioned Farley Salmon, his quarterback on the 8-1 team of '48, to scout the Terrapins. As the date for the game neared, Vaught, Salmon, and defensive coach Buster Poole pulled out the projector to study films of the Eastern powerhouse. Hour after hour, they watched the same material over and over until finally "the boring ritual paid off."

REBELS

They realized that before he took the snap, Maryland's quarterback looked at the opposite way he was going to run. They also saw that the Terp defensive line used the offensive line's splits to determine how it set up.

Vaught used that knowledge to draw up a game plan to attack Maryland on both sides of the ball. The result was a 21-14 upset that made *Newsweek* magazine and netted athletic director Tad Smith a phone call from Sugar Bowl officials while he was still in the locker room after the game. The Associated Press dubbed the Rebel win the No. 1 upset of the year in all sports.

And it all started because the Rebels knew something.

They knew in the same way you know certain things in your life. That your spouse loves you, for instance. That you are good at your job. That tea should be iced and sweetened. That a bad day fishing is still better than a good day at work. You know these things even though no mathematician or philosopher can prove any of this on paper.

It's the same way with faith in Jesus: You just know that he is God's son and the savior of the world. You know it in the same way that you know Ole Miss is the only team worth pulling for: with all your heart, your mind, and your soul.

You just know, and because you know him, Jesus knows you. And that is all you really need to know.

Finally it came through.
-- Farley Salmon on watching Maryland films

A life of faith is lived in certainty and conviction:
You just know you know

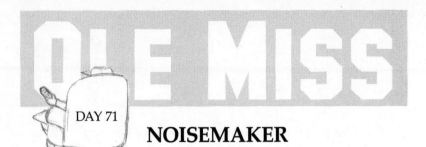

NOISEMAKER

Read Psalm 100.

"Shout for joy to the Lord, all the earth!" (v. 1)

Forty minutes of steady screams." That's the atmosphere in which Ole Miss and Memphis played in the 2010 NIT. For the Rebels, the crowd noise made all the difference down the stretch.

The two teams and their fans certainly preferred playing in the NCAA Tournament. When they met on March 19 in the second round of the NIT, however, the Rebs and the Tigers found themselves playing in a championship-type environment.

Blue-clad Memphis fans filled the upper level of Tad Smith Coliseum while the bottom ring was pretty much all Rebel red. The result was constant noise at a level that made it impossible to tell which team was winning the game.

The two teams played virtually even the first half with Ole Miss grabbing a 37-33 lead at the break. They again played even for much of the last half; the Rebs led 52-47 with about five minutes to play. That's when Ole Miss found an extra burst of energy -- in part from the crowd.

"Certainly the emotion was in the building," said Rebel head coach Andy Kennedy. "No question we got some energy off of the crowd."

The Rebels exploded to put the game away. Memphis turned the ball over three times and went 1-for-4 from the field over a 4:45 stretch. Zach Graham stripped the ball and turned it into a layup. Chris Warren got a steal and converted a reverse layup on the other hand. You can imagine what that did to the crowd noise. But wait, there's more!

Murphy Holloway and Terrico White followed up with a pair of thundering alley-oop dunks. By now, the crowd was out of its mind and Memphis was out of the game. The Rebels won 90-81, becoming only the third UM team in history to win 23 games.

Whether you're at an Ole Miss game live or watching on TV, no doubt you've contributed to the crowd noise generated by thousands of fans or just your buddies. You've probably been known to whoop it up pretty good at some other times in your life, too. The birth of your first child. The concert of your favorite band. That fishing trip when you caught that big ole bass.

But how many times have you ever let loose with a powerful shout to God in celebration of his love for you? Though God certainly deserves it, he doesn't require that you walk around waving pompoms and shouting, "Yay, God!" He isn't particularly interested in having you arrested as a public menace.

No, God doesn't seek a big show or a spectacle. A nice little "thank you" is sufficient when it's delivered straight from the heart and comes bearing joy. That kind of noise carries all the way to Heaven; God hears it even if nobody else does.

When you have a crowd like that, it allows you to sustain the energy from someone other than yourself.
-- Andy Kennedy on the Memphis crowd noise

The noise God likes to hear is a heartfelt "thank you," even when it's whispered.

WITH ALL YOUR HEART

Read Mark 12:28-34.

"Love the Lord your God with all your heart and with all your soul and with all your mind and with all your strength" (v. 30).

As difficult as it is to believe today, football at Ole Miss once nearly disappeared because of a lack of enthusiasm on campus for the game.

After two successful seasons in 1893 and '94 in which the team rolled up a 10-2 record, the school's football program ran into trouble. The students demanded more games on campus. They had simply "tired of building bonfires in Oxford for victories on the foreign fields of Memphis, New Orleans and Jackson."

When the Athletic Association met on Sept. 12, 1895, it acted on the students' request by studying the situation. What it came up with was "empty hands." The association was broke; it didn't have enough money to pay teams to come to Oxford.

The money problems were exacerbated by games such as that of Oct. 27, 1894, in Jackson against Alabama. The *Clarion* reported that more than 1,000 persons attended the game but the gate receipts totaled only $180. A hopeful writer said the freeloaders "can hunt up the cashiers and pay their half dollar without any trouble. No doubt they will do it." No doubt they didn't do it.

With no money and waning interest, team manager William Cook had trouble getting eleven players for a team in 1895. "No

REBELS

one seemed to care whether we had [a football team] or not, and this state of indifference was enough to kill football in any college," wrote *University Magazine.*

But Cook and a few others did care enough to schedule a game on Oct. 12, 1895, against St. Thomas Hall, a prep school. When the University won, student interest suddenly rekindled. A student rally on Oct. 25 raised enough money to keep the program alive.

What fills your life, your heart, and your soul so much that you sometimes just can't help what you do? We all have zeal and enthusiasm for something, whether it's Ole Miss football, sports cars, our family, scuba diving, or stamp collecting.

But do we have a zeal for the Lord? We may well jump up and down, scream, holler, even cry – generally making a spectacle of ourselves – when the Rebels score. Yet on Sunday morning, if we go to church at all, we probably sit there showing about as much enthusiasm as we would for a root canal.

Of all the divine rules, regulations, and commandments we find in the Bible, Jesus made it crystal clear which one is number one: We are to love God with everything we have. All our heart, all our soul, all our mind, all our strength.

If we do that, our zeal and enthusiasm will burst forth. We just won't be able to help ourselves.

For awhile, the outlook for a football team, worthy to represent this University on the gridiron, was very gloomy.
                              -- University Magazine *in 1895*

**The enthusiasm with which we worship God
reveals the depth of our relationship with him.**

WORRYWART

Read Matthew 6:25-34.

"Therefore I tell you, do not worry about your life, what you will eat or drink; or about your body, what you will wear" (v. 25a).

Ole Miss head coach Billy Brewer spent the week worrying. He had a lot to worry about.

Brewer's worry centered on the game of Nov. 12, 1983, against the Tennessee Volunteers. His Rebels had won three in a row, but he worried whether they could keep up with the 6-2 Vols.

He worried about whether his team could handle the pressure of the game. It would be played in Knoxville before more than 95,000 screaming, orange-clad Volunteers fans whose primary mission that night would be to rattle the Rebs. The game was also to be played in prime time and broadcast around the country.

Brewer's response to his worry was a sensible one. He worked to prepare his team, and he prayed. But still, he worried.

He was certainly worried once the game got under way. The Vols drove 58 yards for a touchdown the first time they touched the football. With 9:41 to go in the first quarter, Tennessee was apparently off and running.

As it turned out, Brewer did all that worrying for nothing.

Neil Teevan's 43-yard field goal cut into the Tennessee lead with 2:59 left in the first quarter. The Rebs then used thirteen plays on their next possession to score. Kelly Powell's 4-yard TD pass

REBELS

to split end Jamie Holder was set up by tight end Steve Joyner's catch and rumble to the 5. A second Teevan field goal before the half gave the Rebs a 13-7 lead at halftime.

It stood up as Ole Miss pulled off a 13-10 shocker. Brewer was probably still worried right on up until the last 35 seconds of the game. That's when safety Roger Clark put an end to his coach's worries by nabbing his second interception of the night, shutting down Tennessee's last threat.

"Don't worry, be happy," Jesus admonishes, which is easy for him to say. He never had a mortgage payment to meet or had teenagers in the house. He was in perfect health, never had marital problems, and knew exactly what he wanted to do with his life.

The truth is we do worry. And in the process we lose sleep, the joy in our lives, and even our faith. To worry is to place ourselves in danger of destroying our health, our relationships with those we love, and even our relationship with God. No wonder Jesus said not to worry.

Being Jesus, he doesn't just offer us a sound bite; he gives us instructions for a worry-free life. We must serve God and not the gods of the world, we must trust God and not ourselves, and we must seek God's kingdom and his righteousness.

In other words, when we use our lives to take care of God's business, God uses his love and his power to take care of ours.

If you don't like to worry, why do it? It won't help your performance.
-- Joe Namath

Worrying is a clear sign we are
about our own business rather than God's.

THE BIG TIME

Read Matthew 2:19-23.

"He went and lived in a town called Nazareth" (v. 23).

Jennifer Gillom's basketball career took her all the way from a pasture to a palace.

Gillom grew up about as far from the big time as a youngster could be: Abbeville, Miss., population 419, according to the 2010 census. When the kids got together to play some basketball, they didn't exactly have a nice gymnasium to play in, so they used what they had. "It was a cow pasture," Gillom recalled. "That's where we decided to put our basketball goal."

That humble beginning served Gillom well. The competition was mostly guys, and they pushed her to develop her trademark fadeaway jumper so they couldn't block her shot. "I'd go home every night and take a bath and it was black from the dirt," she remembered.

Gillom's journey to the big-time began in earnest when she arrived in Oxford in 1982. A 6-3 post player, she ended her career at Ole Miss in 1986 as the program's second-leading scorer. (Her sister Peggie (1976-80) is the all-time leading scorer.) As a senior, she was the SEC female athlete of the year and an All-American.

During Gillom's four years in Oxford, the Rebels were 103-23 and won three SEC West titles. Twice they made it to the Sweet Sixteen, and twice they advanced to the Elite Eight.

Her career just kept getting bigger after she graduated. She played pro basketball and was inducted into the Women's Basketball Hall of Fame in 2009. She was a member of the gold-medal U.S. team at the 1988 Olympics in Seoul.

And in 2000, Gillom completed the move from the pasture to the palace when the women's sports complex at Ole Miss was renamed the Gillom Sports Center to honor both Peggie and her.

The move to the big time that Jennifer Gillom made is one we often seek to emulate in our own lives. Bumps in the road, one-stoplight burgs, and villages with nothing but a convenience store, a church, and a voting place dot the American countryside. Maybe you were born in one of them and grew up in a virtually unknown village in a backwater county. Perhaps you started out on a stage far removed from the bright lights of Broadway, the glitz of Hollywood, or the halls of power in Washington, D.C.

Those original circumstances don't have to define or limit you, though, for life is more than geography. It is about character and walking with God whether you're in the countryside or the city.

Jesus certainly knew the truth of that. After all, he grew up in a small town in an inconsequential region of an insignificant country ruled by foreign invaders.

Where you are doesn't matter. What you are does.

We didn't realize we were playing on dirt. We could've been playing in Madison Square Garden.
-- Jennifer Gillom on her beginnings

Where you live may largely be the culmination
of a series of circumstances;
what you are is a choice you make.

LANGUAGE BARRIER

Read Acts 2:1-21.

"Divided tongues, as of fire, appeared among them, and a tongue rested on each of them. All of them were filled with the Holy Spirit and began to speak in other languages, as the Spirit gave them ability" (vv. 3-4 NRSV).

The Rebels first postseason game featured a referee who gave his decisions in both Spanish and English, and they sometimes suffered in translation.

Despite a 3-6 record in 1921, the Rebs accepted an invitation to come to Havana for a game on New Year's Eve against the Cuban Athletic Club. Coach R.L. Sullivan gave each of his sixteen players 50 cents to spend on the train ride to New Orleans. "I took $8 to spend in Havana," recalled future hall-of-famer Calvin Barbour, "but it cost more than 50 cents to eat on the way to New Orleans."

They boarded a ship and set out on Dec. 23 -- and most of the passengers promptly got seasick. Barbour was among those who suffered no ill effects, and he declared, "It was a lovely trip. We had nice sleeping quarters on the second deck -- two men to a room. We were supreme people." In Havana, the Rebel boys had a grand old time. "The Cubans took us all over Havana," said Johnny Montgomery, also a future Ole Miss hall-of-famer.

Game day was sunny and warm, and the powerful Cuban team won 14-0, but a little home cooking may have helped. The Rebs scored three touchdowns, "but they didn't let them count,"

Barbour said. "We were always offside, holding or something."

The referee contributed to the confusion about the rules by relaying his decisions in Spanish to the Cubans and in English to the Mississippians. No one was ever sure that the confusion in language didn't contribution to the confusion in the officiating.

While our games don't always translate across national and cultural boundaries, it is language that usually erects a barrier to understanding. Recall your overseas vacation or your call to a tech support number when you got someone who spoke English but didn't understand it. Talking loud and waving your hands doesn't facilitate communication; it just makes you look weird.

Like many other aspects of life, faith has its jargon that can sometimes hinder understanding. Sanctification, justification, salvation, Advent, Communion with its symbolism of eating flesh and drinking blood – these and many other words have specific meanings to Christians that may be incomprehensible, confusing, and downright daunting to the newcomer or the seeker.

But the heart of Christianity's message centers on words that require no explanation: words such as hope, joy, love, purpose, and community. Their meanings are universal because people the world over seek them in their lives. Nobody speaks that language better than Jesus.

Kindness is the universal language that all people understand.
-- Legendary Florida A&M Coach Jake Gaither

Jesus speaks across all language barriers
because his message of hope and meaning
resounds with people everywhere.

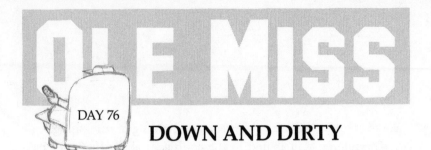

DOWN AND DIRTY

Read Isaiah 1:15-20.

"Though your sins are like scarlet, they shall be as white as snow; though they are red as crimson, they shall be like wool" (v. 18).

Field conditions for the 1967 Egg Bowl were so bad that one writer described the last half as "two quarters of mud wrestling."

When the Rebels and the Bulldogs met in Starkville on Dec. 2, 1967, "half of Scott Field was under water. The other half was a slippery, sloppy mess." A pregame torrential rain evolved into an afternoon of showers and rendered the field one long mudhole.

Both head coaches agreed the conditions were the worst they had ever played in. Uniforms were quickly so muddy that "Ole Miss's white shirts were almost as dark as State's maroon. Numbers were practically illegible." With lightning flashing all morning long, many fans chose to stay away. The smallest crowd in twenty-two years -- only about 21,000 -- braved the weather.

Their tenacity was rewarded as despite the mud and the rain, the two teams put on what was called "a battle royal."

The Rebels took the opening kickoff and drove 28 yards for a field goal. Van Brown booted the 38-yarder just five minutes into the game. The Rebs then acted as though they were playing on a sun-drenched field by marching 47 yards for a touchdown. Senior quarterback Bruce Newell hit high-school teammate J.M. (Mac) Haik with a 7-yard pass for the score. When Brown added the extra point, Ole Miss was up 10-0.

In the mud, that was enough. State's only score came on a field goal after a blocked punt. In the last half, the mud prevailed; the only scoring threats were a pair of missed field goals. Ole Miss won 10-3.

Maybe you've never slopped any pigs and thus have never traipsed around a hog wallow. You may not be a big fan of mud boggin'. Still, you've worked on your car, planted a garden, played touch football in the rain, or endured some military training. You've been dirty.

Dirt, grime, and mud aren't the only sources of stains, however. We can also get dirty spiritually by not living in accordance with God's commands, by doing what's wrong, or by not doing what's right. We all experience temporary shortcomings and failures; we all slip and fall into the mud.

Whether we stay there or not, though, is a function of our relationship with Jesus. For the followers of Jesus, sin is not a way of life; it's an abnormality, so we don't stay in the filth. We seek a spiritual bath by expressing regret and asking for God's pardon in Jesus' name. God responds by washing our soul white as snow with his forgiveness.

An athlete's journey towards perfection is often times paved with mud, blood, sweat, and tears.
— Paralympic gold medal winner Sarah Will

**When your soul gets dirty, a powerful and
thorough cleansing agent is available
for the asking: God's forgiveness.**

TEACHER'S PET

Read John 3:1-16.

"[Nicodemus] came to Jesus at night and said, 'Rabbi, we know you are a teacher who has come from God'" (v. 2).

Two-time NCAA national champion Brittney Reese was such a natural talent that she was the state high school track and field athlete of the year pretty much without any coaching.

Reese was a really good basketball player in high school when one hot spring day of her junior year, a coach promised her a cold drink if she would take a shot at the long jump. "Having no clue about proper form or where to land or even what to do," she gave it a try. When she landed, the coach's eyes lit up. Containing his excitement, he calmly asked, "Why don't you go try that again?" She did and landed in pretty much the same spot. Reese's life was forever changed.

Basketball was her first love, and so she didn't have any time to devote to track. She simply showed up for meets and jumped. She had such natural jumping abilities that she was the state's 2004 Gatorade track and field athlete of the year, excelling despite not having any personal training.

She played basketball for two seasons at Gulf Coast Community College, which didn't have a track program. Ole Miss track coach Joe Walker then offered her a track scholarship, even though she had never been coached and hadn't jumped in two years.

With a little coaching and teaching and a lot of running, Reese

REBELS

blossomed into a world-class athlete, her jumps getting longer and longer. "She looked like she might be good," said fellow Ole Miss jumper Jasmine Dacus. "But then the girl just blew up."

Reese was the NCAA Outdoor Champion in the long jump in both 2007 and 2008 and competed in the 2008 Summer Olympics in Beijing. In 2009 in Berlin, she won the world championship.

Brittney Reese was a natural, but a little teaching and coaching made her a champion.

You can read this book, break 90 on the golf course, and do your job well because somebody taught you. And as you learn, you become the teacher yourself. You teach your children how to play Monopoly and how to drive a car. You show rookies the ropes at the office and teach baseball's basics to a Little League team.

This pattern of learning and then teaching includes your spiritual life also. Somebody taught you about Jesus, and this, too, you must pass on. Jesus came to teach a truth that the religious teachers and the powerful of his day did not want to hear. Little has changed in that regard, as the world today often reacts with scorn and disdain to Jesus' message.

Nothing, not even death itself, could stop Jesus from teaching his lesson of life and salvation. So should nothing stop you from teaching life's most important lesson: Jesus saves.

I can dunk.

-- Brittney Reese on her natural jumping abilities

**In life, you learn and then you teach,
which includes learning and teaching about Jesus,
the most important lesson of all.**

DAY 78

SEEING THE VISION

Read Acts 26:1, 9-23.

"So then, . . . I was not disobedient to the vision from heaven" (v. 19).

Johnny Vaught had a vision of what it would take to field a winning football team at Ole Miss. Acting on that vision, Vaught changed Southern college football permanently.

When Vaught joined the Ole Miss staff as an assistant in 1946, he was under no illusions. "Ole Miss offered a coaching challenge," he said. That challenge remained when he was named head coach in '47. So did the vision Vaught had brought east with him from Texas. "When I shook [athletic director] Tad Smith's hand and accepted the head coach's job, all thoughts that Ole Miss was a coaching graveyard had been put out of my mind," Vaught said.

Vaught admitted he "was a Texan in the wilderness" and "had a hard time adjusting to the conditions." After all, as he put it, "The athletic facilities in 1946 were pitiful." The athletic office was one room in an old gym. When he met with his assistant coaches, they had to stand around or sit on steps. "We often sat in cars for our football staff meetings," Vaught recalled.

The heart and soul of Vaught's vision for winning football at Ole Miss was playing with home-grown talent. Assembling his first coaching staff, he interviewed a former Ole Miss football and baseball player named Tom Swayze, who was at the time a high-school coach. He didn't get the job he sought, but when Swayze arrived for the interview, he came with two possible recruits. Duly impressed, Vaught hired him as the first full-time recruiter in the South, the man directly responsible for channeling that home-grown talent to Oxford.

Swayze's success over the next 25 years meant that in the 1950s and '60s, "no SEC or national championship could be considered without first factoring in Ole Miss." It also meant that recruiters became a staple of college football coaching staffs everywhere.

To speak of visions is often to risk their being lumped with palm readings, Ouija boards, seances, horoscopes, and other such useless mumbo-jumbo. The danger such mild amusements pose, however, is very real in that they indicate a reliance on something other than God. It is God who knows the future; it is God who has a vision and a plan for your life; it is God who has the answers you seek as you struggle to find your way.

You probably do have a vision for your life, a plan for how it should unfold. It's the dream you pursue through your family, your job, your hobbies, your interests. But your vision inspires a fruitful life only if it is compatible with God's plan. As the apostle Paul found out, you ignore God's vision at your peril. But if you pursue it, you'll find an even more glorious life than you could ever have envisioned for yourself.

I knew Ole Miss could win with its share of Mississippi boys.
  -- Johnny Vaught on his vision of winning football at Oxford

**Your grandest vision for the future pales
beside the vision God has of what the two of you
can accomplish together.**

DIVIDED LOYALTIES

Read Matthew 6:1-24.

"No one can serve two masters" (v. 24a).

Ole Miss or Mississippi State? Loyalties aren't divided in the Magnolia State. You're either for one or the other with no in-between. Except for the case of Breck Tyler, who has experienced the Egg Bowl as no one else ever has.

Tyler grew up on both sides of the rivalry. In 1968, he was 10 years old and a staunch Ole Miss fan as his father, Bob, was a Rebel assistant that season. "It was what put the food on the table," he said, "and Mississippi State was the enemy." He attended every Ole Miss practice and walked the Rebel sideline during games. His hero was record-setting split end Floyd Franks, and Archie Manning threw him passes.

When he was 16, his dad was the head coach in Starkville. He attended every State practice and caught passes from Rockey Felker. He played for the Bulldogs and his dad in 1977 and '78, but when his dad resigned, he went back to his old ways, even if they were somewhat schizophrenic. He transferred to Ole Miss and played for the Rebels in 1980 and '81. Swapping those particular uniforms was a little strange. "When I ran out on that field dressed as a Rebel, that was an extremely unique feeling," he said.

As a result, historians declare that Tyler, who played wide receiver and led the Rebels in receiving in 1980, is the only player in modern football history to play for both schools in the Egg

REBELS

Bowl. Reflecting his divided loyalties, in his office in downtown Jackson was an unusual sight: On a shelf side by side were both an Ole Miss and a Mississippi State helmet.

For Tyler, the divided loyalty carries no bitterness for either side. "It's the people and the relationships that mean the most now," he said. His most poignant memory of the Egg Bowl came in 1980 when he suffered an injury. He was wearing a Rebel uniform, but it was State players who helped him up and off the field.

Like Breck Tyler, you understand the stress that results from divided loyalties. The Christian work ethic drives you to be successful. The world, however, often makes demands and presents images that conflict with your devotion to God: movies deride God; couples play musical beds in TV sitcoms; and TV dramas portray Christians as killers following God's orders.

It's Sunday morning and the office will be quiet or the golf course won't be crowded. What do you do when your heart and loyalties are pulled in two directions? Jesus knew of the struggle we face; that's why he spoke of not being able to serve "two masters," that we wind up serving one and despising the other. Put in terms of either serving God or despising God, the choice is stark and clear.

Your loyalty is to God -- always.

You're not going to get that out of me.
-- Breck Tyler, when asked whom he pulls for in the Egg Bowl

**God does not condemn you for being successful
and enjoying popular culture, but your loyalty
must lie first and foremost with him.**

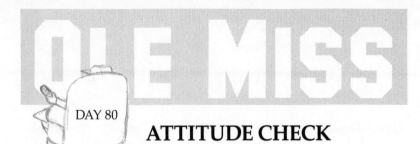

ATTITUDE CHECK

Read 1 Thessalonians 5:12-22.

"Give thanks in all circumstances, for this is God's will for you in Christ Jesus" (v. 18).

While hard work and talent had much to do with it, a good part of the reason for the Rebels' turnaround in 2008 had to do with a change in attitude.

The first time he met with his players, new head coach Houston Nutt asked how many of them had ever played in a bowl game. "And not one guy could raise their hand," he recalled. So he made every player promise the seniors they would play in a bowl game that year. And thus the change in attitude began.

A lot needed to be changed. When Nutt and his staff took over after the 2007 season, thirty-three players were academically ineligible and many were out of shape. Offensive line coach Mike Markuson called them "fat slobs." The entire team was described as "demoralized, beaten down by four straight losing seasons."

Nutt set out to end the losing but also to put some light into the players' lives. On the practice field and in the hallways, he met his players with a smile and words of encouragement. "We went from night and now it's day," said offensive lineman John Jerry.

But even Nutt the optimist was tested. After the Rebs fumbled six times against Vanderbilt, the last at the Commodore 1, and fell to 3-4, even the head coach experienced some negative vibes. "It seems like we've got the perfect recipe of finding a way to lose,"

REBELS

he told his wife. "It was deeper rooted than I thought."

But the attitude change was also deeper rooted than Nutt might have thought. Instead of folding, the Rebels recovered. They won six straight games and fulfilled that pre-season promise made to the seniors by thumping 8th-ranked Texas Tech in the Cotton Bowl. (See Devotion No. 14.)

"God put [Nutt] into our lives for a reason," said senior receiver Mike Wallace. "I'm glad I had one year of a positive experience with these coaches."

How's your attitude? You can fuss because your house is not as big as some, because a coworker talks too much, or because you have to take pills every day. Or you can appreciate your home for providing warmth and shelter, the co-worker for the lively conversation, and the medicine for keeping you reasonably healthy.

Whether life is endured or enjoyed depends largely on your attitude. An attitude of thankfulness to God offers you the best chance to get the most out of your life because living in gratitude means you choose joy in your life no matter what happens. This world does not exist to satisfy you, so chances are it will not. True contentment and joy are found in a deep, abiding relationship with God, and the proper way to approach God is not with haughtiness or anger but with gratitude for all he has given you.

Everybody's positive, every single person on the staff.
-- Receiver Mike Wallace on the attitude in 2008

Your attitude goes a long way
toward determining the quality of your life
and of your relationship with God.

THE GREATEST

Read Mark 9:33-37.

"If anyone wants to be first, he must be the very last, and the servant of all" (v. 35).

Take it to the bank as fact: Chris Warren is the greatest free-throw shooter in SEC history.

The 5-10 point guard finished his Rebel career in 2011 as one of the greatest players in school history. He set school records for 3-point field goals made (334) and attempted and consecutive games with a 3-pointer made (46). He is third in school history in career points. He was first-team All-SEC his senior season, a year in which he became only the fourth player in SEC history with 2,000 points and 400 assists. (LSU's Pete Maravich, Tennessee's Allan Houston, and Georgia's Litterial Green are the others.) In his four years in Oxford, Warren started every game in which he played; the only exception was Senior Day his freshman year.

Despite all the accolades and honors that came his way, Warren will forever be known for his prowess at the free-throw line. In 2011, he led the NCAA in and set both the Ole Miss and the SEC records for free-throw accuracy by hitting 92.8 percent of his charity shots. The previous record-holder was Kentucky's Kyle Macy, who hit 91.2 percent of his free throws in 1980.

Warren was virtually automatic from the line. Fellow guard Zach Graham, who set a school record by playing in 135 games, said once he had never seen Warren miss two free throws in a row at practice. When teammates would make fun of Warren to lure him into missing a few, it never worked. "He'll be laughing while he's shooting them and still hitting them," Graham said.

Head coach Andy Kennedy agreed with Graham's description, calling Warren "unflappable" on the court and at the line. Warren credited his success to technique, not changing his routine ever, always repeating the big ball-spin and the dramatic knee bend.

The results didn't change either; he was, after all, the greatest.

We all want to be the greatest. The goal for the Rebels and their fans every season is the national championship. The competition at work is to be the most productive sales person on the staff or the Teacher of the Year. In other words, we define being the greatest in terms of the struggle for personal success. It's nothing new; Jesus' disciples saw greatness in the same way.

As Jesus illustrated, though, greatness in the Kingdom of God has nothing to do with the secular world's understanding of success. Rather, the greatest are those who channel their ambition toward the furtherance of Christ's kingdom through love and service, rather than their own advancement, which is a complete reversal of status and values as the world sees them.

After all, who could be greater than the person who has Jesus for a brother and God for a father? And that's every one of us.

When he gets on the free-throw line, everyone expects it to go in.
-- Andy Kennedy on Chris Warren

To be great for God has nothing to do
with personal advancement and everything to do
with the advancement of Christ's kingdom.

FRIENDS FOREVER

Read Ecclesiastes 4:9-12.

"If one falls down, his friend can help him up. But pity the man who falls and has no one to help him up!" (v. 10)

They were the odd couple of SEC football: an Auburn strong safety and an Ole Miss running back who became friends because they collided in a violent tackle during a game. And one basically saved the other's life.

On Oct. 31, 2009, with 2:42 left in the first quarter, freshman Rebel tailback Rodney Scott collided with Auburn strong safety Zac Etheridge and Tiger linebacker Eltoro Freeman. Freeman got to his feet at once after the play; Scott normally would have done the same. This time, though, he lay flat on his back, and he had Etheridge across him. He could not feel the Auburn player moving at all. "When he made no effort to get up, I just stayed as still as I could," Scott said.

The trainers came out and asked Scott if he were hurt, and he told them he wasn't. When they asked Etheridge, he didn't say anything, though he was conscious. But he couldn't move. All he could do was whisper a barely audible prayer while the huge crowd went silent and players from both teams knelt to pray. "All I could say was 'Jesus, Jesus,'" Etheridge remembered. "I just kept calling His name over and over."

For ten minutes, Scott remained deathly still himself while Etheridge was strapped to a backboard. He had torn neck ligaments and a fractured vertebra, injuries that ended his season but did not threaten either his career or his life. Doctors called Scott a hero and told him that had he made any movement, Etheridge could well have been left paralyzed.

Before long, the two SEC warriors were chatting and keeping up with each other, what may well be a lifelong friendship the unexpected result of a potential tragedy.

Lend him your car or some money. Provide tea, sympathy, and comfort him when she's down. Talk him out of a bad decision. What wouldn't you do for a good friend?

We are wired for friendship. Our psyche drives us to seek both the superficial company of others that casual acquaintance provides and the more meaningful intimacy that true friendship furnishes. We are perhaps at our noblest when we selflessly help a friend.

So if we wouldn't think of turning our back on our friends, why would we not be the truest, most faithful friend of all by sharing with them the gospel of Jesus Christ? Without thinking, we give a friend a ride, but we know someone for years and don't do what we can to save her from eternal damnation. Apparently, we are quite willing to spend all of eternity separated from our friends. What kind of lousy friend is that?

It is kind of weird, but personally I need to stay in touch with the guy who basically saved my life.
-- Auburn's Zac Etheridge on his friendship with Rodney Scott

**A true friend introduces a friend
to his friend Jesus.**

THE 'I' IN PRIDE

Read 1 John 2:15-17.

*"Everything in the world -- the desire of the flesh, the
desire of the eyes, the pride in riches -- comes not from the
Father but from the world" (v. 16 NRSV).*

The best season in football history to that time led to a resur-
gence of pride in the Ole Miss program in 1935. What practically
everyone wasn't proud of, however, was the team's nickname.

With a 9-3 record, Coach Ed Walker's sixth team was a bona fide
powerhouse. The backfield star was senior halfback Rab Rodgers,
a three-year letterman who became known as the Tupelo Ghost.
The season saw the emergence of tackle Frank "Bruiser" Kinard,
the school's first All-American.

In the wake of the unprecedented season, grumbling about the
school's nickname -- the Flood -- increased. An alternative -- the
Red and Blue -- had surfaced, but it was too unwieldly for newspaper headline writers to use.

The sports editor of the campus newspaper called the football
team "a man without a country, a child without a home" with "no
real nickname with which to be properly identified." He asked
sports editors from around the South to spread the word about a
search for a new name and soon had more than six hundred suggestions, including Raiders, Confederates, Stonewalls, and simply
Ole Miss. History credits alumnus Ben Guider as being the first to
suggest the Mississippi Rebels. Twenty-one sports editors voted

REBELS

from a list pared down by a committee to five names; eighteen of them chose the Rebels.

On July 10, 1936, the faculty committee on athletics -- by a slim 4-3 margin -- voted to let the football team be known as the Ole Miss Rebels, a name they felt everyone could be proud of.

What are you most proud of? The size of your bank account? The trophies from your tennis league? The title under your name at the office? Your family?

Pride is one of life's great paradoxes. You certainly want a surgeon who takes pride in her work or an Ole Miss coach who is proud of his team's accomplishments. But pride in the things and the people of this world is inevitably disappointing because it leads to dependence upon things that will pass away and idolization of people who will fail you. Self-pride is even more dangerous because it inevitably leads to self-glorification.

Pride in the world's baubles and its people lures you to the earthly and the temporary, and away from God and the eternal. Pride in yourself yields the same results in that you exalt yourself and not God.

God alone is glorious enough to be worshipped. Jesus Christ alone is Lord.

Southerners are proud of their football heritage, their schools, and their teams. And they share a deep pride that goes with being from the South.
-- Announcer George Mooney

Pride can be dangerous because it tempts you
to lower your sight from God and the eternal
to the world and the temporary.

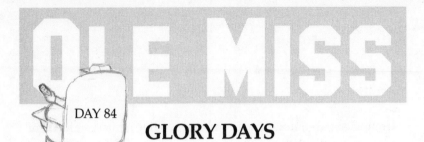

DAY 84

GLORY DAYS

Read Colossians 3:1-4.

"When Christ, who is your life, appears, then you also will appear with him in glory" (v. 4).

Whatever happens to Ole Miss football in the future, Rebel fans can always cling tightly to the memory of the glorious days from 1959-63 when only a pair of close losses to LSU kept the Rebs from five straight undefeated seasons.

By 1959, Johnny Vaught had established a true dynasty in Oxford. As the '59 season began, the Rebs had already experienced the most glorious days in the program's history to that point. They had won SEC titles in 1947, '54, and '55; they had had seven straight seasons of at least seven wins and had set a school record in '55 with ten wins. "The Rebels had moved to the top of college football's mountains," said one writer. "High school stars came by the truckload" to Oxford. As Ole Miss guard Warner Alford, a co-captain of the 1960 team, put it, "There weren't any bad days. Losing never crossed our mind."

But that stretch of excellence only laid the groundwork for the five years of glory that began in '59. 9-1-0, 9-0-1, 9-1-0, 9-0-0, 7-0-2 -- those were the regular-season records, a total of 43-2-3. The Rebs finished in the top ten each season and won three SEC championships and three national titles, the latter according to various polls in the days before a BCS game. The Associated Press judged the 1959 team to be the SEC's Team of the Decade.

REBELS

Nine Rebels received All-American recognition during these glory days: guard Marvin Terrell, quarterback Jake Gibbs, end Johnny Brewer, fullback Billy Ray Adams, offensive lineman Jim Dunaway, guard Treva Bolin, quarterback Doug Elmore, quarterback Glynn Griffing, and center-linebacker Kenny Dill.

You may well remember the play that was your moment of athletic glory. Or the night you received an award from a civic group for your hard work. Your first (and last?) ace on the golf course. Your promotion at work. Your first-ever 10K race. Life does have its moments of glory.

But they amount to a lesser, transient glory, which actually bears pain with it since you cannot recapture the moment. The excitement, the joy, even the happiness – they are fleeting; they pass as quickly as they arose, and you can never experience them again.

Glory days that last forever are found only through Jesus. That's because true glory properly belongs only to God, who has shown us his glory in Jesus. To accept Jesus into our lives is thus to take God's glory into ourselves. Glory therefore is an ongoing attribute of Christians. Our glory days are right now, and they will become even more glorious when Jesus returns.

The real glory is being knocked to your knees and then coming back. That's real glory. That's the essence of it.

-- Vince Lombardi

**The glory of this earth is fleeting,
but the glory we find in Jesus lasts forever
– and will only get even more magnificent.**

CALLING IT QUITS

Read Numbers 13:25-14:4.

"The men who had gone up with him said, 'We can't attack those people; they are stronger than we are'" (v. 13:31).

A rules change and a bunch of babies led directly to a pair of bad seasons that left Johnny Vaught giving serious thought to quitting at Ole Miss early in his career.

Vaught began his Oxford career with two sensational seasons in 1947 (9-2 and the SEC title) and '48 (8-1). Two-platoon football burst onto the scene in 1949, though, and Ole Miss was not ready. "It takes 44 pretty good boys to play the game with unlimited substitution, and Ole Miss could not meet such a manpower demand then," Vaught said.

Vaught's whole coaching philosophy had been built around the best athlete he could find, a star who played both offense and defense. Such a player was fullback Kayo Dottley, who was the leading rusher and scorer in the SEC in 1949. Now the game called for one-way athletes, specialists; Ole Miss didn't have them.

And then there were the weddings, which created a different sort of "platoons" problem for the head coach. As he put it, "Ole Miss players were having children by platoons." Vaught was convinced that togetherness was a key factor in molding a successful team. He was also convinced that all the marriages and the babies that soon showed up hurt that togetherness. After the 1950 season, he offered scholarships only to unmarried athletes, a decision, he said, that "helped to put Ole Miss on the road to better football."

The 1949 and '50 seasons were a combined 9-10-1 that left the coach depressed and considering leaving. He decided he didn't have the luxury of crying and that he didn't want to be known as a quitter. His grandmother wouldn't have liked it either.

And so he stayed. The rest is Ole Miss legend as Vaught never had another losing season.

Remember that time you quit a high-school sports team? That night you bailed out of a relationship? Walked away from a job with the goals unachieved? Sometimes quitting is the most sensible way to minimize your losses, so you may well at times in your life give up on something or someone.

In your relationship with God, however, you should remember the people of Israel, who quit when the Promised Land was theirs for the taking. They forgot one fact of life you never should: God never gives up on you.

That means you should never, ever give up on God. No matter how tired or discouraged you get, no matter that it seems your prayers aren't getting through to God, no matter what – quitting on God is not an option.

He is preparing a blessing for you, and in his time, he will bring it to fruition -- if you don't quit on him.

It was the only time I seriously considered leaving Ole Miss.
– Johnny Vaught on the tough 1949-50 seasons

Whatever else you give up on in your life, don't give up on God; he will never ever give up on you.

SMILING FACES

Read Philippians 4:4-7.

"Rejoice in the Lord always. I will say it again: Rejoice!"
(v. 4)

As Johnny Vaught once put it, "Laughter is part of the Mississippi mystique." He had the stories to prove it.

For instance, during preparations for the 1961 Sugar Bowl (a 14-6 defeat of Rice), second-string halfback Frank Halbert told Vaught that his folks wanted to be in New Orleans when the team arrived. So he asked the head coach, "What time are we going to get there?" Vaught hadn't named the traveling squad, so he glared hard at Halbert and asked, "What do you mean, we?" "Well, coach," Halbert replied, "you are going too, aren't you?" After Vaught quit laughing, he put Halbert on the traveling squad.

A locker room ritual that always elicited a whole lot of smiles and laughter involved longtime team physician Ferrell "Doc" Varner, a charter member of the Ole Miss Athletics Hall of Fame. The players developed a rather unique way of celebrating Varner's birthday each year: They gave him money -- usually $100 or so -- and threw him into the whirlpool. Naturally, this was a noisy, joyous ritual.

You would think Varner appreciated the money but didn't too much care for the dousing. One year, though, the players gave him the cash but forget about the bath. So Varner spent a few minutes stomping around the locker room muttering until the players remembered. They promptly threw him into the water.

The players once pulled a memorable joke on their coach, who admitted he had to be firm and fair but didn't believe in starched collars. In El Paso for the '67 Sun Bowl, Vaught was about to speak at a luncheon when a woman wearing a gown "with a low neck that fairly well exposed her" ran up to him and declared loudly that he had left his game notes in her room the night before. As the room -- especially the players -- roared with laughter, the coach quickly realized he had been had.

What does your smile say about you? What is it that makes you smile and laugh in the first place? Your dad's corny jokes? Don Knotts as Barney Fife? Your children or grandchildren? Your pal's bad imitations? Do you hoard your smile or do you give it away easily even when you've had some tough times?

When you smile, the ones who love you and whom you love can't help but return the favor -- and the joy. It's like turning on a bright light in a world threatened by darkness. Besides, you have good reason to walk around all the time with a smile on your face not because of something you have done but rather because of one basic, unswerving truth: God loves you. As a result of his great love for you, God acted through Jesus to give you free and eternal salvation. That should certainly make you smile.

A laugh is better than a fistfight when competition for a starting slot is fierce or a game is close.

-- Johnny Vaught

It's so overused it's become a cliché, but it's true nevertheless: Smile! God loves you.

HOMEBODIES

Read 2 Corinthians 5:1-10.

"We . . . would prefer to be away from the body and at home with the Lord" (v. 8).

An Ole Miss All-America once traded a mansion for a jail cell -- and he was quite happy about it.

Barney Poole was an All-American end who played both sides of the ball at Ole Miss in 1942 and then in 1947 and '48 after a stint with Army during World War II. He was named to the Ole Miss Team of the Century and was inducted into the College Football Hall of Fame in 1974 in addition to the Mississippi Sports and Ole Miss Athletic halls of fame.

Poole grew up on a farm near Gloster, which boasted a population of 1,100. One afternoon, a coach from Natchez watched in dismay as his basketball team lost to the Gloster country boys. He was especially impressed by Poole, the team's best player. Poole had never played football because his school was too small to field a team, but the coach had a proposal for him.

If the youngster would come to Natchez to play with the coach and his teams, he would find him a place to stay. That seemed like a pretty good deal to Poole, so he went. He was quickly back home in Gloster, though, because the home the coach had found for him didn't suit him at all. It was "practically a suite" in one of the city's famous antebellum homes.

Poole said the place "was too rich for my country blood." So he "packed up and went home where I could walk around in my bare feet if I felt like it."

The persistent coach chased Poole down and told him he had another place for him. This one suited Poole just fine. It was a private cell in the Adams County jail. "Got three good meals a day and could do almost as I pleased," Poole said.

The squatter got evicted, though, when an audit revealed that the jail had been dishing out more meals than it had prisoners. The ingenious coach found Poole another place to his liking: a room over an old drug store.

Home is not necessarily a matter of geography. It may be that place you share with your spouse and your children, whether it's Mississippi or Alaska. You may feel at home when you return to Oxford, wondering why you were so eager to leave in the first place. Maybe the home you grew up in still feels like an old shoe, a little worn but comfortable and inviting.

God planted that sense of home in us because he is a God of place, and our place is with him. Thus, we may live a few blocks away from our parents and grandparents or we may relocate every few years, but we will still sometimes feel as though we don't really belong no matter where we are. We don't; our true home is with God in the place Jesus has gone ahead to prepare for us. We are homebodies and we are perpetually homesick.

Everybody's better at home.
— *Basketball player Justin Dentmon*

**We are continually homesick for our real home,
which is with God in Heaven.**

UNBELIEVABLE

Read Hebrews 3:7-19.

*"See to it, brothers, that none of you has a sinful,
unbelieving heart that turns away from the living God"*
(v. 12).

What Ole Miss pulled off in the second quarter of the 1971 Egg
Bowl remains to this day simply unbelievable.

Billy Kinard's first season at the helm was a rousing success.
The Rebs went 10-2, beat LSU, and stomped Georgia Tech 41-18 in
the Peach Bowl. And then there was the Egg Bowl.

The two teams slugged it out on pretty equal terms for three
quarters with the Rebels managing only a 6-0 edge on a pair of
field goals from Cloyce Hinton. Those other fifteen minutes, however -- they were the ones that were so unbelievable.

After a scoreless first quarter came what the *Memphis Commercial Appeal* called 9:27 of "football hysteria." During that stretch,
the Rebels scored an unbelievable 42 points on six touchdowns
and six extra points.

The carnage began with a State punt that set Ole Miss up at the
Bulldog 23. On the fifth play, tailback Greg Ainsworth scored the
first of his three TDs. Hinton kicked the extra point.

Fourteen seconds later, the score was 14-0. Henry Walsh forced
a fumble that Reggie Dill recovered, and Ainsworth scored on
the first play. Only two plays later, Dill recovered another fumble.
Quarterback Norris Weese fired a 28-yard TD strike to tight end

REBELS

Burney Veazey two plays later.

Then came a 60-yard drive and a three-play drive after another Bulldog fumble (Weese to split end Riley Myers for a 35-yard score). The points orgy ended when defensive back Stan Moley took an interception 43 yards for a touchdown. 42-0.

The unbelievable quarter mercifully ended 75 seconds later before Ole Miss had time to score again.

What we claim not to believe in reveals much about us. UFOs. Global warming. Sasquatch. Aluminum baseball bats. The BCS.

Most of what passes for our unbelief has little effect on our lives. Does it matter much that we don't believe a Ginsu knife can stay sharp after repeatedly slicing through tin cans? Or that any other team besides Ole Miss is worth pulling for?

That's not the case, however, when Jesus and God are part of the mix. Quite unbelievably, we often hear people blithely assert they don't believe in God. Or brazenly declare they believe in God but don't believe Jesus was anything but a good man and a great teacher.

At this point, unbelief becomes dangerous because God doesn't fool around with scoffers. He locks them out of the Promised Land, which isn't a country in the Middle East but Heaven itself.

Given that scenario, it's downright unbelievable that anyone would not believe.

Football is so incredible sometimes it's unbelievable.

-- Tom Landry

Perhaps nothing is as unbelievable as that some people insist on not believing in God or his son.

DEAD WRONG

Read Matthew 26:14-16; 27:1-10.

"When Judas, who had betrayed him, saw that Jesus was condemned, he was seized with remorse" (v. 27:3).

Kentucky head coach Bear Bryant stated he didn't believe "any team with freshmen could beat me." A ref signaled touchdown. A sportswriter sent out a bulletin saying Kentucky beat Ole Miss. They were all wrong.

The advent of two-platoon football in 1949 hit Ole Miss hard. After a 17-3 record and an SEC championship over the last two seasons, the Rebels fell to 4-5-1 in 1949 and 5-5 in 1950. "Ole Miss simply was not ready for two-platoon football," declared head coach Johnny Vaught. That was because the new substitution rules "called for a lot of manpower," and Ole Miss didn't have it. Only twenty-one lettermen reported in the fall of 1949.

In 1951, though, Vaught and his coaches caught up by playing freshmen. That left the Rebs extremely young, eliciting the Bear's disdainful comment prior to the game in Oxford. The coaches made sure the statement showed up on the Rebel information sheet distributed to the players before the game. Bryant had good reason to be confident, though; his Cats were 20-point favorites.

But one of those freshmen, wingback Lea Pasley, committed Bryant's remark to memory and was determined to prove the coach wrong. He did his part, throwing a 28-yard touchdown pass to junior end Bud Slay for the game's first score. The contest turned into a thriller that was not decided until the last play.

Kentucky appeared to have saved itself on a pass into the end zone; one official even signaled touchdown. But Rebel linebacker Pete Mangum blasted the receiver, who dropped the ball. That didn't keep a sportswriter from prematurely firing off a bulletin that said Kentucky had won 23-21.

But he was wrong and so was the Bear. A Rebel team with freshmen on it pulled off the 21-17 upset.

There's wrong, there's dead wrong, and there's Judas wrong. We've all been wrong in our lives, but we can at least honestly ease our conscience by telling ourselves we'll never be as wrong as Judas was. A close examination of Judas' actions, however, reveals that we can indeed replicate in our own lives the mistake Judas made that drove him to suicidal despair.

Judas ultimately regretted his betrayal of our Lord, but his sorrow and remorse, however boundless, could not save him. His attempt to undo his initial wrong was futile because he tried to fix everything himself rather than turning to God in repentance and begging for mercy.

While we can't literally betray Jesus to his enemies as Judas did, we can match Judas' failure in our own lives by not turning to God in Jesus' name and asking for forgiveness for our sins. In that case, we ultimately will be as dead wrong as Judas was.

There's nothing wrong with the car except that it's on fire.
-- Formula One racing commentator Murray Walker

A sin is the first wrong; failing to ask God
for forgiveness of it is the second.

AT A LOSS

Read Philippians 3:1-9.

"I consider everything a loss compared to the surpassing greatness of knowing Christ Jesus my Lord, for whose sake I have lost all things" (v. 8).

Armintie Price played her senior season at Ole Miss with a heart broken by loss.

Price is a Rebel basketball legend. As a senior in 2007, she led the Rebels to the Elite Eight. She was tops on the team in scoring, rebounds, assists, and steals. Her 3.7 steals per game led the nation. She is the only guard ever to lead the SEC in rebounding and joined Cheryl Miller as the only players in NCAA history to amass 2,000 points, 1,000 rebounds, 400 assists, and 400 steals.

"My mom was my life," Price once said. She had to get permission from her mother before she could even play basketball. A devout Pentecostal, her mother relented only upon the condition that her daughter wear a skort, a combination of skirt and shorts. This bypassed the faith's ban on girls wearing pants. Price wore the skort in track too while she won fifteen state titles.

When she prepared to head to Oxford, Price told her mother, "I still love God. I want to be saved. But I don't want to wear a skort." She received the maternal dispensation.

As Price was leaving a summer class and preparing to drive home in 2006, she received the shattering news that her mother had died at 49 of ovarian cancer. A few days after her mother was buried, she left a team meeting to cry. She thought, "I need a year off. I can't deal with this." But then she thought, "Momma would whup my behind if I ever thought about taking a year off."

After all, this was a woman who raised five children as a single parent working fast-food jobs. "She was a fighter," Price said. So Price fought too, with a magnificent senior season during which she often sang and talked to her mother. "It doesn't feel weird to me," she said.

Maybe, as it was with Armintie Price, it was when a member of your family died. Perhaps it wasn't so staggeringly tragic: your puppy died, your best friend moved away, or an older sibling left home. Sometime in your youth or early adult life, though, you learned that loss is a part of life.

Loss inevitably diminishes your life, but loss and the grief that accompanies it are part of the price of loving. When you first encountered loss, you learned that you were virtually helpless to prevent it or escape it.

There is life after loss, though, because you have one sure place to turn. Jesus shares your pain and eases your suffering; but he doesn't stop there. Through the loss of his own life, he has trans-formed death -- the ultimate loss -- into the ultimate gain of eternal life. In Jesus lies the promise that one day loss itself will die.

I talk to God and Mom and ask for guidance and help.
-- Armintie Price during her senior season

Jesus not only eases the pain of our losses
but transforms the loss caused by death
into the gain of eternal life.

DAY 91

RUN FOR IT

Read John 20:1-10.

"Peter and the other disciple started for the tomb. Both were running, but the other disciple outran Peter and reached the tomb first" (vv. 3-4).

What the first football coach at Ole Miss did that marked the official start of football practice startled quite a few of Oxford's more curious housewives: He had the team go for a run.

The father of football at Ole Miss is Dr. Alexander Lee Bondurant, a professor of Greek and Latin whose interest in sports led him to organize the school's first football team in 1893. (See Devotion No. 1) He had discovered football in 1892 while he was doing graduate work at Harvard.

Back in Oxford in the early autumn of 1893, the thin, mustachioed, 28-year-old professor presented the idea of a university football team to a student assembly. Not a one of the school's 173 students had ever played the game. Nevertheless, the students received the proposal enthusiastically despite (or because of?) faculty protestations that the game was too rough. The most earnest of the students decided to forge ahead with a team.

A few days later, at 6:30 a.m. at the school's old latticed gymnasium, Bondurant gathered thirty aspiring football players and led them on a four-mile run, which caused some consternation in the sedate Oxford community. According to Bondurant, who apparently was quite pleased with himself for the commotion he

REBELS

created, "It shocked the conservatism of many of the old land-marks of Oxford to see a troop of men, led by a professor scantily clad, running through the streets of the town."

Not a single student finished the run. Ten left what had been dubbed by another professor as "Bondurant's fool football team." The next morning, though, twenty students returned. Senior law student Alfred Roudebush, who would be the first team's captain, told Bondurant, "Professor, we will see the season through."

He promptly put them through thirty minutes of exercise and then led them on another four-mile run.

Every morning you hit the ground running as you leave the house and re-enter the rat race. You run errands; you run though a presentation; you give someone a run for his money; you always want to be in the running and never run-of-the-mill.

You're always running toward something, such as your goals, or away from something, such as your past. Many of us spend much of our lives foolishly attempting to run away from God, the purposes he has for us, and the blessings he is waiting to give us.

No matter how hard or how far you run, though, you can never outrun yourself or God. God keeps pace with you, calling you in the short run to take care of the long run by falling to your knees and running for your life -- to Jesus -- just as Peter and the other disciple ran that first Easter morning.

On your knees, you run all the way to glory.

I never get tired of running. The ball ain't that heavy.
                                                                    -- Herschel Walker

You can run to eternity by going to your knees.

WINNER'S CIRCLE

Read 1 John 5:1-12.

"Who is it that overcomes the world? Only he who believes that Jesus is the Son of God" (v. 5).

We don't care about the glory. We want wins." Spoken like a true offensive lineman.

Ole Miss guard Marcus Johnson issued that pithy viewpoint common to all offensive linemen. He spoke shortly after the Rebel offensive line prevented what would have been the biggest collapse in Ole Miss football history.

On Nov. 1, 2003, the 20th-ranked Rebs routed the South Carolina Gamecocks for 43 minutes. The offense piled up 538 yards with Eli Manning throwing for 391 yards, Tremaine Turner rushing for 117 yards, and wide receiver Chris Collins catching ten passes for 125 yards.

The lead went to 43-14 in the third quarter behind the seven-man rotation the Rebels used in the offensive line: Tre Stallings, Cliff Woodruff, and Bobby Harris at tackle; center Justin Sawyer; Johnson and Doug Buckles at guard; and Chris Spencer backing up all three positions.

But then, as one writer put it, "the Rebels got sloppy and lost their focus." USC scored on the last play of the third quarter and added three more touchdowns. With 1:40 to play, Ole Miss led only 43-40 and had the ball at its own 31. Carolina had a pair of timeouts left. Knowing what was coming, the Gamecock defense

REBELS

bunched up at the line to stop the run. That's just what they got; thanks to the offensive line, it didn't matter.

Turner got four yards on first down and five yards on second down. Needing only one yard for the win that would keep them undefeated in the SEC, the Rebs relied on their line. Manning got two on a quarterback sneak behind Sawyer.

This time the offensive linemen got the glory and the win.

Life itself, not just athletic events, is a competition. You vie against other job or college applicants. You compete against others for a date. Sibling rivalry is real; just ask your brother or sister.

Inherent in any competition or in any situation that involves winning and losing is an antagonist. You always have an opponent to overcome, even if it's an inanimate video game, a golf course, or even yourself.

Nobody wants to be numbered among life's losers. We recognize them when we see them, and maybe mutter a prayer that says something like, "There but for the grace of God go I."

But one adversary will defeat us: Death will claim us all. We can turn the tables on this foe, though; we can defeat the grave. A victory is possible, however, only through faith in Jesus Christ. With Jesus, we have hope beyond death because we have life.

With Jesus, we win. For all of eternity.

Winning means you're willing to go longer, work harder, and give more than anyone else.

-- Vince Lombardi

Death is the ultimate opponent;
Jesus is the ultimate victor.

COMEBACK KIDS

Read Acts 9:1-22.

"All those who heard him were astonished and asked, 'Isn't he the man who raised havoc in Jerusalem among those who call on this name?'" (v. 21)

By today's standards, a twelve-point comeback in the last half of a college basketball game doesn't seem all that sensational. But how about such a rally in 1928 to win a championship?

Ole Miss began its varsity basketball program on Jan. 28, 1909, with a game against the Memphis Physicians from the medical school. The game was played outdoors on a court behind the Lyceum on the Ole Miss campus. The Mississippians, as they were then known, led 7-6 at the half but lost 12-11.

Ole Miss joined the Southern Conference in 1922, one year after its formation. The program's first run at the title came in 1926 with a team that won twelve straight, a school record that stood until the 2007-08 team won thirteen straight. They lost to North Carolina in the tournament's championship game.

The Mississippians of coach Homer Hazel made a more successful run at the title in 1928, but it required a sensational comeback. The team went into the league tournament in Atlanta with only a 6-9 record, but they won three straight to advance to the finals and were barely tested in the process. They whipped NC State 40-35, LSU 55-28, and Kentucky 41-28.

Lying in wait in the finals were the Auburn Tigers, whom the

Oxford boys had nudged 43-42 in their first meeting. Auburn had blasted them 58-38, however, in a rematch.

This game appeared headed the way of that last encounter when Auburn led 25-13 in the second half. But then captain Robert M. Lee, described by the yearbook as "the long, lanky leader of the Mississippians," rallied the team to a stirring comeback that netted a 31-30 win and the program's first league title.

Life will have its setbacks whether they result from personal failures or from forces and people beyond your control. Being a Christian and a faithful follower of Jesus Christ doesn't insulate you from getting into deep trouble. Maybe financial problems suffocated you. A serious illness put you on the sidelines. Or your family was hit with a great tragedy.

Life is a series of victories and defeats, and winning isn't about avoiding defeat; it's about getting back up to compete again. It's about making a comeback of your own.

When you avail yourself of God's grace and God's power, your comeback is always greater than your setback. You are never too far behind, and it's never too late in life's game for Jesus to lead you to victory, to turn trouble into triumph. As it was with the Mississippians in the 1928 Southern Conference Tournament and with Paul, it's not how you start that counts; it's how you finish.

Many [of the spectators] were a bit sorry for Ole Miss and hoped they would make just a few more points so as not to be humiliated.
-- Ole Miss yearbook on the crowd before the comeback vs. Auburn

In life, victory is truly a matter of how you finish and whether you finish with Jesus at your side.

LIVE ACTION

Read James 2:14-26.

"Faith by itself, if it is not accompanied by action, is dead"
(v. 17).

Tennessee talked. Ole Miss played ball.

As strange as it sounds, Ole Miss' battle against Tennessee in 1969 actually began in August. That's when a Vol linebacker shot off his mouth, saying he wasn't impressed with Archie Manning's arm. When a writer suggested that Ole Miss had the horses to challenge for the league title, the player responded, "I think they have mules."

Aware of the danger of giving an opponent such ammunition, the Tennessee head coach had someone tell the player to say he had just been joking. The player refused.

His ill-conceived words were permanent fixtures in the Rebel locker room that fall. "By game time, the Rebels were frothing." They weren't exactly alone; "the campus and an entire state were in a frenzy awaiting the Vols." A mule showed up on campus that week, bearing a "Squeeze the Orange" sign.

On Nov. 15, the third-ranked Vols showed up in Jackson and discovered to their sorrow that talk without action is worthless.

The Rebels took the opening kickoff and marched right down the field, using only 4:29 to score. A pass from Manning to junior split end Floyd Franks to the Vol 3 set up Manning's TD run. The capacity crowd "stared in disbelief at the ease of the Rebel score."

REBELS

It never really got any tougher for the Rebels. They led 21-0 after the first quarter and went on to win 38-0. Middle guard Larry Thomas led a defense that forced four turnovers and allowed the Vols a total of 259 yards. It was the worst loss Tennessee had endured since 1923. One columnist called the Rebel performance "the best all-around team effort we've ever witnessed."

The Rebs did their talking after the game. Manning declared Ole Miss was a good team at every position. "I guess we proved it today," he said. Sophomore tailback Randy Reed got in a jab at the injudicious Volunteer: "He really is a big mouth."

Talk is cheap. Consider your neighbor or coworker who talks without saying anything, who makes promises she doesn't keep, who brags about his own exploits, who can always tell you how to do something but never shows up for the work.

How often have you fidgeted through a meeting, impatient to get on with the work everybody is talking about doing? You know – just as Tennessee learned against Ole Miss -- that speech without action just doesn't cut it.

That principle applies in the life of a person of faith too. Merely declaring our faith isn't enough, however sincere we may be. It is putting our faith into action that shouts to the world of the depth of our commitment to Christ. Just as Jesus' ministry was a virtual whirlwind of activity, so are we to change the world by doing.

Jesus Christ is alive; so should our faith in Him be.

Man, we're gonna kill them for what they've said.
-- Ole Miss lineman prior to '69 Tennessee game

Faith that does not reveal itself in action is dead.

GOOD LUCK

Read Acts 1:15-25.

"Then they prayed, 'Lord, you know everyone's heart.
Show us which of these two you have chosen.' . . . Then
they cast lots" (vv. 24, 25a).

My luck ain't going too good right now." It didn't get much better for Ole Miss defensive end Greg Hardy.

Hardy rendered his dour assessment of his luck prior to the 2009 football season, his last for Ole Miss. He was All-SEC as a sophomore in 2007 with ten sacks -- which led the league -- and eighteen tackles for a loss. He had also played a season with the basketball team and had scored three touchdowns as a wide receiver. Even then, though, Hardy's luck wasn't all good; he was suspended for two games by head coach Ed Orgeron, who was looking for an attitude adjustment.

Then before the 2008 season, he broke a small bone in his foot that required surgery to repair. He hurried back and played well at first. Gradually, though, he faded and wasn't really much of a factor, playing in only six games. Old questions about his attitude and effort returned, but what was limiting Hardy was not his mind but his foot.

So in January before his senior season, he had a second surgery. He was on track to be at full speed for fall drills when teammate Dexter McCluster and he were involved in a wreck. The accident aggravated the injury, and Hardy wound up in a walking cast.

As the 2009 season neared, though, he was optimistic that his run of bad luck was over. He shouldn't have been. He reinjured the ankle in the season opener and was relegated primarily to third-down situations. Still, his five sacks were leading the team when a fractured left wrist finished his season and his career.

Hardy did finally have some good luck when the Carolina Panthers took him in the sixth round of the 2010 draft.

Ever think that other people have all the luck? Some guy wins a lottery while you can't get a raise of a few lousy bucks at work. The football takes a lucky bounce the other team's way and Ole Miss loses a game. If you have any luck to speak of, it's bad.

To ascribe anything that happens in life to blind luck, however, is to believe that random chance controls everything, including you. But here's the truth: There is no such thing as luck, good or bad. Even when the apostles in effect flipped a coin to pick the new guy, they acknowledged that the lots merely revealed to them a decision God had already made.

It's true that we can't explain why some people skate merrily through life while others suffer in horrifying ways. We don't know why good things happen to bad people and vice versa. But none of it results from luck, unless you want to attribute that name to the force that does indeed control the universe; you know -- the one more commonly called God.

Luck is what happens when preparation meets opportunity.
-- Darrell Royal

A force does exist that is in charge,
but it isn't luck; it's God.

BE PREPARED

Read Matthew 10:5-23.

"I am sending you out like sheep among wolves. Therefore be as shrewd as snakes and as innocent as doves" (v. 16).

The season before, Kentucky had shut down the Ole Miss offense with its defensive strategy. Now, though, first-year Rebel head coach Johnny Vaught had his team prepared.

Vaught won the school's first SEC title in football in 1947, his first year on the job. It was no accident; neither were any of his 190 wins. Vaught was the Boy Scout of football coaches; his motto was "Be Prepared." He even turned down a Sunday TV show so he could stay in Oxford and begin preparing for the next game.

At TCU, Vaught played for a coach who once ran the same play seventy-two times in practice. An exhausted, exasperated player let the air out of the coach's tires in retaliation.

Vaught studied game films as few had before him. He wanted his scouts to emulate Mike Brumbelow, of whom it was said, he "could tell Vaught how many knots a player had in his shoelaces."

Not surprisingly, therefore, Vaught had his Rebels prepared for his first game as head coach, the 1947 season opener against Bear Bryant's Kentucky Wildcats. In 1946, Bryant's defense had confused the Ole Miss offensive linemen by jumping around at the last moment. To combat the movement and minimize the confusion, Vaught drilled guards Jimmy Crawford and Bernard Blackwell to the point that they could instantly shout out the defense after the Wildcats made their last move.

The preparation showed. Ole Miss won 14-7, outgained the Cats 233-166, and protected quarterback Charley Conerly so well he completed fifteen passes. Vaught heaped praised upon his whole line after the game: Blackwell, Crawford, Bill Erickson, David Bridgers, George Lambert, and Everette Harper.

You know the importance of preparation in your own life. You went to the bank for a car loan, facts and figures in hand. That presentation you made at work was seamless because you practiced. The kids' school play didn't suffer any embarrassing meltdowns because they rehearsed. Knowing what you need to do and doing what you must to succeed isn't luck; it's preparation.

Jesus understood this, and he prepared his followers by lecturing them and by sending them on field trips. Two thousand years later, the life of faith requires similar training and study. You prepare so you'll be ready when that unsaved neighbor standing beside you at your backyard grill asks about Jesus. You prepare so you will know how God wants you to live. You prepare so you are certain in what you believe when the secular, godless world challenges it.

And one day you'll see God face to face. You certainly want to be prepared for that.

[Johnny] Vaught was at his best in preparation.
-- Johnny Bruce, who played under three coaches at Ole Miss

Living in faith requires constant study
and training, preparation for the day
when you meet God face to face.

FOUND WANTING

Read Psalm 73:23-28.

*"Whom have I in heaven but you? And earth has nothing
I desire besides you" (v. 25).*

What Rebel head baseball coach Mike Bianco wanted most of
all was to avoid using his bullpen in the 2009 regional championship game. Drew Pomeranz made sure he got what he wanted.

The 42-18 Rebels, the SEC co-champs with LSU, took on 42-
19 Western Kentucky in the finals of the regional in Oxford. Bianco fully expected to use his bullpen in that game since the
Hilltoppers had scored 36 runs on 59 hits in their four games in
the regional. They had banged out twenty hits against the Rebs
the day before to force the winner-take-all championship game.
Moreover, Pomeranz was pitching with only two days' rest.

But the left-handed sophomore threw a masterpiece, striking
out a school-record-tying sixteen batters. He took a no-hitter
into the seventh inning and finished by giving up only two hits,
neither of which left the infield. Most importantly for his head
coach, Pomeranz threw a complete game.

"That was a legendary performance by Drew Pomeranz," Bianco said. "We talked about it and knew it in our coaches' meeting
this morning that he was capable of a Curt Schilling-bloody sock
moment."

He was, but Western Kentucky still had a shot at winning the
game and ending the Rebel season. Ole Miss led only 1-0 in the

top of the seventh when the Hilltoppers got their first hit on a grounder that was bobbled in the infield. Two outs later, an infield single chased home the tying run.

But first baseman Matt Smith drilled a two-run triple that sent the Rebs on their way to a 4-1 win. It also kept Pomeranz on the mound and on the way to his complete game. Which was just what Mike Bianco wanted.

What do you want out of life? A loving, caring family, a home of your own, the respect of those whom you admire? Our heart's desires can elevate us to greatness and goodness, but they can also plunge us into destruction, despair, and evil. Drugs, alcohol, control, sex, power, worldly success: Do these motivate you?

Desires are not inherently evil or bad for you; after all, God planted the capacity to desire in us. The key is determining which of your heart's desires are healthful and are worth pursuing and which are dangerous and are best avoided.

Not surprisingly, the answer to the dilemma lies with God. You consult the one whose own heart's desire is for what is unequivocally best for you, who is driven only by his unqualified love for you. You match what you want for yourself with what God wants for you. Your deepest heart's desire must be the establishment and maintenance of an intimate relationship with God.

An awesome attitude is best described as a "bad case of the wants."
-- Former football coach Erk Russell

Whether our desires drive us to greatness or to destruction is determined by whether they are also God's desires for our lives.

PROBLEM CHILD

Read James 1:2-12.

*"Blessed is the man who perseveres under trial, because
when he has stood the test, he will receive the crown of life
that God has promised to those who love him" (v. 12).*

Ole Miss punter Jim Miller was so good that he caused all sorts
of problems.

Miller, a barefoot punter from 1976-79, led the NCAA in punt-
ing as a sophomore with a 45.9-yard average. That broke the SEC
record of 45.3 yards, which had been set by the Rebels' own Charley Conerly. Miller also set a school record with an 82-yard kick
against South Carolina in 1977. He was inducted into the Ole Miss
Athletics Hall of Fame in 1995.

Miller booted the ball long and high, which created sensational
hang time and a real problem for Mike Pope, the Rebels' kicking
and offensive-line coach. Pope discovered that Miller's kicks
were so long and so high that his coverage team, "staffed with the
normal allotment of lumbering offensive linemen," couldn't get
downfield fast enough to cover the punts and prevent returns. He
solved the problem by loading the punt team up with six defensive backs, two wide receivers, and two running backs.

Miller's booming kicks also created another problem. In pre-
game warmups for the 1978 season opener, a crowd showed up
just to watch him kick and cheer him on. "He was airmailing the
thing, and the people were applauding," Pope said. To please the

enthusiastic fans, Miller punted more than his usual allotment of fifteen kicks. "He may have kicked himself out," Pope said because Miller's first kick in the game was short and was returned for a touchdown. "He does attract a crowd, so we have to watch him," Pope said.

It was, though, a nice problem for the Rebels to have.

Problems are such a ubiquitous feature of our lives that a whole day – twenty-four hours – without a single problem ranks right up there with a government without taxes, a Rebel team that never loses a game, and entertaining, wholesome television programs. We just can't even imagine it.

But that's life. Even Jesus had his share of problems, especially with his twelve-man staff. Jesus could have easily removed all problems from his daily walk, but what good would that have done us? Our goal is to become like Jesus, and we could never fashion ourselves after a man who didn't encounter job stress, criticism, loneliness, temptation, frustration, and discouragement.

Instead, Jesus showed us that when – not if – problems come, a person of faith uses them to get better, rather than letting the problems use him to get bitter. We learn God-filled perseverance and patience as we develop and deepen our faith and our trust in God. Problems will pass; eternity will not.

The problem with winter sports is that they take place in winter.
-- Humorist Dave Barry

The problem with problems is that
we often let them use us and become bitter
rather than using them to become better.

CLOTHES HORSE

Read Genesis 37:1-11.

"Israel loved Joseph more than all his children, because he was the son of his old age: and he made him a coat of many colours" (v. 3 KJV).

Two of Ole Miss' earliest football coaches had some issues with clothes during their tenures in Oxford.

Bill Driver came down from Missouri in 1913 to head up the Rebel program. One of the more radical causes for which he campaigned was the use of numbered jerseys. Prior to the 1913 game against Cumberland (won by Ole Miss 7-0), Driver and his captain, Forrest McCall, proposed the squads wear numbered uniforms. Cumberland declined, saying the idea was silly. At least one newspaper was on Driver's side, declaring, "The teams of the effete East have refused to number their athletes, offering the ridiculous and inadequate excuse that such an innovation served to commercialize the sport."

Driver eventually won out, though. On Oct. 17, 1914, the Rebels defeated LSU 21-0 in Baton Rouge with both teams wearing numbered jerseys.

In the fall of 1918, head coach Dudy Noble took one look at a scrawny freshman student who turned out for football and said, "Rat, we don't have anything you can wear." The freshman, who stood 5-8 and weighed all of 135 pounds, responded that he would take any scraps the coach had, so the two rounded up

REBELS

enough odd pieces to suit him up. When the player walked out onto the practice field in his get-up, team captain Edward Ray asked, "Where did this scarecrow come from?"

The "scarecrow" was Calvin Barbour, who went on to earn four letters in football and five in baseball. He was captain of the 1922 team and a charter member of the Ole Miss Athletics Hall of Fame.

Contemporary society proclaims that it's all about the clothes. Buy that new suit or dress, those new shoes, and all the sparkling accessories, and you'll be a new person. The changes are only cosmetic, though; under those clothes, you're the same person. Consider Joseph, for instance, prancing about in his pretty new clothes; he was still a spoiled little tattletale whom his brothers detested enough to sell into slavery.

Jesus never taught that we should run around half-naked or wear only second-hand clothes from the local mission. He did warn us, though, against making consumer items such as clothes a priority in our lives. A follower of Christ seeks to emulate Jesus not through material, superficial means such as wearing special clothing like a robe and sandals. Rather, the disciple desires to match Jesus' inner beauty and serenity -- whether the clothes the Christian wears are the sables of a king or the rags of a pauper.

I cannot agree with coach Haughton of Harvard, who said numbers would give a squad the aspect of a chain gang.
-- Bill Driver in support of jersey numbers

**Where Jesus is concerned,
clothes don't make the person; faith does.**

THE END

Read Revelation 22:1-17.

"I am the Alpha and the Omega, the First and the Last, the Beginning and the End" (v. 13).

The most successful era in Ole Miss football history -- that led by the team of athletic director Tad Smith and head coach Johnny Vaught -- came to an end with the 1970 season.

On the job since 1947, Vaught staggered as he was leaving the athletic dorm cafeteria the Tuesday before the Vanderbilt game of 1970. "Coach, you're tripping over everything," said assistant coach Billy Mustin. Vaught shrugged off the episode and went back to work. Later that evening, though, he finally told his staff, "Boys, I'm sick. I've got to go home."

Vaught drove the five miles to his home and crawled into bed. Soon, though, he told his wife, "There's something wrong with me." There was indeed; Vaught was seriously ill with a heart problem. He listened to the game that Saturday, the 250th of his Rebel career, from a hospital bed. After a week, he left the hospital eager to rejoin his team, but during his second night at work, the pain returned. This time, he wound up in intensive care in Memphis.

As his illness improved, Vaught, who was only 61, decided he wanted to continue coaching. He signed a new four-year contract in November. Smith signed a one-year extension.

But in January 1971, Vaught's doctor told him that a return to coaching was not an option, that the stress could be fatal. "I resented the fact that illness was forcing me out," Vaught said. "I had never even had a bad headache before this thing."

So he left his doctor and went to Smith's office in the athletic department to deliver the bad news to the man who had hired him and joined him to make up the most formidable team in Ole Miss history -- and in the SEC -- during their tenure. The end of that great era officially came on Jan. 21, 1971, when Billy Kinard was hired as the 27th head football coach at Ole Miss.

The successful Smith-Vaught era in Ole Miss football is just another example of a basic truth: Everything ends. Even the stars have a life cycle, though admittedly it's rather lengthy. Erosion eventually will wear a boulder to a pebble. Life itself is temporary; all living things have a beginning and an end.

Within the framework of our individual lifetimes, we meet endings. Loved ones, friends, and pets die; relationships fracture; jobs dry up; our health, clothes, lawn mowers, TV sets – they all wear out. Even this world as we know it will end.

But one of the greatest ironies of God's gift of life is that not even death is immune from the great truth of creation that all things must end. That's because through Jesus' life, death, and resurrection, God himself acted to end any power death once had over life. In other words, because of Jesus, the end of life has ended. Eternity is ours for the claiming.

John, if you can't coach I will retire and you can be the athletic director.
-- AD Tad Smith to Johnny Vaught at the end of an era

Everything ends;
thanks to Jesus Christ, so does death

NOTES
(by Devotion Day Number)

1   On Nov. 11, 1893, a group of Baptists, . . . shouting and laughing Mississippians.": William W. Sorrels and
     Charles Cavagnaro, *Ole Miss Rebels* (Huntsville, AL: The Strode Publishers, Inc., 1976), p. 16.
1   For six weeks, a young . . . on the game's fundamentals.: Billy Watkins, *University of Mississippi Football Vault*
     (Atlanta: Whitman Publishing, LLC, 2009), p. 8.
1   He also fed them healthful . . . abide by a 10 p.m. curfew.: Watkins, *Mississippi Football Vault*, p. 9.
1   As the first-ever game day . . . furnished their own shoes: Sorrels and Cavagnaro, p. 17.
1   agreed to be responsible for . . . both these good colleges.": Watkins, *Mississippi Football Vault*, p. 9.
1   An exuberant crowd met the . . . convivially talked things over.: Watkins, *Mississippi Football Vault*, p. 10.
1   the 3 p.m. kickoff: Sorrels and Cavagnaro, p. 17.
1   "Every man did his duty, . . . the performance was rather unusual,": Sorrels and Cavagnaro, p. 17.
1   [Beginning the football program] was . . . who had ever played the game.: Watkins, *Mississippi Football Vault*,
     p. 6.
2   the "Immaculate Deflection.": coined by *Clarion-Ledger* sportswriter Butch John and quoted in William G.
     Barner, *The Egg Bowl* (Jackson: University Press of Mississippi, 2007), p. 251.
2   The Rebs had scored 17 . . . covering only 52 yards.: Barner, p. 250.
2   "It went straight and long . . . Rebel fans went bananas.": Billy Watkins, "Rebels, Mother Nature Stop Bull-
     dogs," *OleMissSports.com*, http://www.olemisssports.com/sports/m-footbl-spec-rel/112808aae.html.
2   It is probably the only field goal ever celebrated by both teams.: Barner, p. 251.
3   Abernethy and Ole Miss head coach . . . abiding relationship with Jesus Christ.: Janet Goreham, "Rebel with
     a Cause," *Sharing the Victory Magazine*, http://www.sharingthevictory.com/vsItemDisplay.lsp?method
     =display&objectid=Ad9A09.
3   the game was always second to his faith.: Goreham, "Rebel with a Cause."
3   everything to do with . . . Fellowship of Christian Athletes.: Goreham, "Rebel with a Cause."
3   I met a lot of strong . . . could grow the most spiritually.: Goreham, "Rebel with a Cause."
4   Only the urging of team . . . two games into the 1945 season.: Sorrels and Cavagnaro, p. 131.
4   "Drew took command of . . . so small they resembled shorts.: Sorrels and Cavagnaro, p. 131.
4   The word soon circulated around . . . jumped up and down and cussed.: Sorrels and Cavagnaro, p. 135.
5   Three offensive linemen went down, . . . was in at right tackle.: Rick Cleveland, "Injuries? Noise? Pressure?"
     Rebel Run (Jackson: The *Clarion-Ledger*/Sports Publishing L.L.C., 2004), p. 134.
5   "a cast of second- and third-team players forced into action at critical stages.": Michael Wallace,
     "6-0: Only One to Go," *Rebel Run* (Jackson: The *Clarion-Ledger*/Sports Publishing L.L.C., 2004), p. 119.
5   senior quarterback Eli Manning had . . . they needed to do.": Wallace, "6-0: Only One to Go," p. 120.
5   He had begun the season . . . longest play of his career.": Wallace, "6-0: Only One to God," p. 119.
5   Our guys found a way.: Wallace, "6-0: Only One to Go," p. 120.
6   The father found his son . . . know if I can make it,": Sorrels and Cavagnaro, p. 249.
6   he would be one of eight . . . we had won the year before,": Watkins, *Mississippi Football Vault*, p. 80.
6   He had always wanted to go . . . to make a decision, I couldn't,": Sorrels and Cavagnaro, p. 249.
6   The father advised his son . . . you shouldn't change it.": Sorrels and Cavagnaro, p. 249.
6   All I needed was for my . . . That made up my mind.: Sorrels and Cavagnaro, p. 249.
7   Lauren Grill is, no doubt, the best of her sport ever to wear red and blue.": Ivory Tower, "The Grove Bracket:
     (1) Eli Manning v. (8) Lauren Grill," *RedCupRebellion.com*, June 1, 2010, http://www.redcuprebellion.
     com/2010/6/1/1454225.
7   "pushed her program as far as anyone before her has.": Tower, "The Grove Bracket."
7   "pretty much everything.": Tower, "The Grove Bracket."
7   she had spent the season hacking . . . over into a patient hitter,: David Brandt, "Grill's New Patience at Plate
     May Lift UM to NCAA Bid," *The Clarion-Ledger*, April 15, 2010, https://secure.pqarchiver.com/clarion
     ledger/access/2009830301.html.
7   If they're not going to . . . what you need to win.: Brandt, "Grill's New Patience at Plate."
8   The two men watched it all . . . in the 1999 Egg Bowl.: Barner, p. 312.
8   The bands jointly played the . . . universities and the governor.: Barner, p. 313, 315.
9   "one of the most physical games I ever played in.": Watkins, *Mississippi Football Vault*, p. 72.
9   The referee had whistled the . . . The crowd was too loud.": Sorrels and Cavagnaro, p. 209.
9   So the teams rehuddled and . . . signaled the kick was good.: Sorrels and Cavagnaro, p. 210.
9   Certainly the ball landed outside the left post.: Sorrels and Cavagnaro, p. 210.
9   Some Arkansas players said they . . . wouldn't have called it good.": Sorrels and Cavagnaro, p. 211.
10   "I always felt he was mistreated in 1929.": Sorrels and Cavagnaro, p. 97.
10   The president of the alumni . . . in all departments of athletics.": Watkins, *Mississippi Football Vault*, p. 23.
10   After a 6-0 loss to . . . to A&M on his watch.: Sorrels and Cavagnaro, p. 89.
10   "Hazel was a hero," . . . and I loved him.": Sorrels and Cavagnaro, p. 97.
10   He "took his firing philosophically" . . . to play for the Rebels.: Sorrels and Cavagnaro, p. 97.
11   Rebel tennis coach Mark Byers . . . could have done any better.": John Holt, "Vlaar Mature Beyond Her
     Years," *The Daily Mississippian*, March 9, 2011, http://www.thedmonline.com/article/vlaar-mature-

beyond-her-years.
11 When I think that I'll . . . it's kind of creepy.: Holt, "Vlaar Mature Beyond Her Years."
12 "We're going to win them all.": Sorrels and Cavagnaro, p. 190.
12 About two hundred disappointed . . . going to win them all.": Sorrels and Cavagnaro, p. 190.
12 Paige Cothren scored five points . . . head coach Wally Butts,: Sorrels and Cavagnaro, p. 190.
13 The 1981 Egg Bowl was a mismatch on paper.: Barner, p. 241.
13 "the wildest ending ever": Francis J. Fitzgerald, ed., *Greatest Moments in Ole Miss Football History* (Birmingham: Epic Sports, 1999), p. 126.
13 "Thousands headed for the exits, thinking that the game was over.": Barner, p. 242.
13 "as the Bulldogs screamed in protest and the Rebels cheered,: Barner, p. 243.
13 The State defender told the . . . kind of pushed me.": Barner, p. 243.
13 The official made the call, and that's that.: Barner, p. 243.
14 In 1936, a Dallas oilman watched . . . a New Year's Day game too.: "Texas Tech, Ole Miss Meet in Cotton Bowl Farewell," *Sporting News*, Jan. 1, 2009, http://aol.sportingnews.com/ncaa-football/story/2009-01-01/texas-tech-ole-miss-meet.
14 "Mom had black-eyed peas . . . to watch the Cotton Bowl,": "Texas Tech, Ole Miss Meet."
14 They did backflips at . . . around carrying ovesized flags.: "Snead, McCluster Lead Ole Miss Past Texas Tech," *Sporting News*, Jan. 2, 2009, http://aol.sportingnews.com/ncaa-football/story/2009-01-02/snead-mccluster-lead-ole-miss.
14 We'll make the announcement . . . next year, right now.: "Snead, McCluster Lead Ole Miss."
15 We did what we had to do to win,": Rick Cleveland, "Rebels Beat State in Overtime," *The Clarion-Ledger*, Jan. 24, 1981, http://www.olemisssports.com/sports/m-baskbl/spec-rel/013009aab.html.
15 Four straight times in the . . . They never got off a shot.: Cleveland, "Rebels Beat State in Overtime."
15 the Rebs held the ball . . . a strike for a layup.: Cleveland, "Rebels Beat State in Overtime."
16 The experts decided Brandon Bolden . . . running backs at Oxford.: Derek Stephens, "The Story of Brandon Bolden," *BleacherReport.com*, April 22, 2009, http://bleacherreport.com/articles/160452-the-story-of-brandon-bolden.
16 He was "far and away" more intense than anyone else on the roster.: Brandon Marcello, "Quiet Leader Bolden Ready to Take Charge as Senior," *The Clarion-Ledger*, July 8, 2011, http://www.clarionledger.com/article/20110708/SPORTS030103/107080335.
16 In the spring of 2011, . . . "Yes, sir, I am.": Marcello, "Quiet Leader Bolden Ready to Take Charge."
16 "ambivalent, vacillating, impulsive, unsubmissive.": John MacArthur, *Twelve Ordinary Men* (Nashville: W Publishing Group, 2002), p. 39.
16 "the greatest preacher . . . in the birth of the church.: MacArthur, p. 39.
16 Anybody can go out there and . . . quiet and lead by example.: Marcello, "Quiet Leader Bolden Ready to Take Charge."
17 "The genial doctor brought . . . University of Mississippi.": Sorrels and Cavagnaro, pp. 56-57.
17 A&M had asked Stauffer to . . . shocked five thousand.: Sorrels and Cavagnaro, p. 64.
17 "Boomalacka, boomalacka, wow . . . rah rah rah!": Sorrels and Cavagnaro, pp. 59, 61.
18 "Taciturn Charles Albert Conerly, . . . the best way I can.": Sorrels and Cavagnaro, p. 152.
18 [Charley Conerly's] quiet confidence . . . anyone in the huddle.: Sorrels and Cavagnaro, p. 156.
19 Junior colleges and small schools . . . scrimmaging with the guys.: Parrish Alford, "McFerrin, a Former Tupelo High Star, Lands Starting Role for Ole Miss," *NEMS360.com*, Feb. 10, 2011, http://nems360.com/view/full_stop/11339451/article."
19 McFerrin got the itch again, . . . "that girl from Tupelo" to Ladner.: Alford, "McFerrin, a Former Tupelo High Star."
19 At her first practice, she . . . "just a walk-on.": Kaitlyn Dubose, "McFerrin Walk-On Turned Starter for Lady Rebs," *The Daily Mississippian*, Feb. 22, 2011, http://www.thedmonline.com/article/mcferrin-walk-turned-starter-lady-rebs.
19 The first time a coach . . . about to go in.": Alford, "McFerrin, a Former Tupelo High Star."
19 I just never thought . . . much less starting. I'm amazed.: Alford, "McFerrin, a Former Tupelo High Star."
20 Billy Brewer described as "slow death.": Butch John, "Ole Miss Holds Off Vanderbilt," *The Clarion-Ledger*, Oct. 23, 1983, http://www.olemisssports.com/sports/m-footbl/spec-rel/091710aaa.html.
21 not at all confident as they prepared to take on Arkansas.: Watkins, *Mississippi Football Vault*, p. 138.
21 "This game was different. . . . . and it was very hard,": "Arkansas Fans Greet Nutt with Boos," *Sporting News*, Oct. 25, 2008, http://aol.sportingnews.com/ncaa-football/story/2008-10-25/arkansas-fans-greet-Nutt-boos."
21 "I've been booed when I was . . . Arkansas' side of the field.: "Rebels Hold On in Nutt's Return to Arkansas," *Sporting News*, Oct. 25, 2008, http://aol.sportingnews.com/ncaa-football/story/2008-10-25/rebels-hold-nutts-return-arkansas.
21 One fan threw an empty . . . been in their living room.: "Arkansas Fans Greet Nutt with Boos."
21 It was harder than I . . . the last four years,": "Rebels Hold On in Nutt's Return."
21 It is hard not to love . . . are close to them.: "Rebels Hold On in Nutt's Return."
22 If I have to play boys that size, I might as well go back to Georgia.": Sorrels and Cavagnaro, p. 126.
22 In 1938, Ike Knox . . . at a whopping 135 pounds,: Sorrels and Cavagnaro, p. 126.
22 Described as "stumpy" and "little,": Sorrels and Cavagnaro, p. 128.
22 "talent that at the least is defined as greatness.: Sorrels and Cavagnaro, p. 128.

23   with a 23-3 lead when they . . . wound up at the five.: Sorrels and Cavagnaro, p. 227.

24   Arkansas head coach Nolan . . . since Rob took over.": Kelli Anderson, "Rebels with a Cause," *Sports Illustrated*, Jan. 20, 1997, http://sportsillustrated.cnn.com/vault/article/magazine/MAG1009379/index.htm.

24   "After you've won the game, . . . he said exactly that,: Anderson, "Rebels with a Cause."

24   The Rebels cracked the top 20 the next week.: Anderson, "Rebels with a Cause."

25   As part of the festivities . . . throw at the Cornhuskers.: Michael Wallace, "Rebels Rule in Real World," *The Clarion-Ledger*, Dec. 28, 2002, p. D1, https://secure.pqarchiver.com/clarionledger/access/1834566511. html.

25   "In the third quarter," . . . They weren't as physical.": Wallace, "Rebels Rule in Real World."

26   "The helmets in those days . . . several games without a helmet.": Sorrels and Cavagnaro, p. 86.

26   In response to the Florida heat, . . . wearing of jerseys in a game.: Sorrels and Cavagnaro, p. 93.

27   "a great team man" . . . "played as hard as he could.": Sorrels and Cavagnaro, p. 158.

27   In the Tulane loss, Poole . . . pointing toward my tonsils.": Sorrels and Cavagnaro, p. 159.

27   One of those who didn't score . . . to put me back in.": Sorrels and Cavagnaro, pp. 159-60.

28   "Chase and I were pretty fast . . . and Lee went along.: Matt Sigler, "Moore Looks to Cap Successful Year at NCAA Championships," *The Daily Mississippian*, June 7, 2011, http://www.thedmonline.com/article/ moore-looks-cap-successful-year-ncaa-championships.

28   "Because I run for the . . . please my father in heaven.": Sigler, "Moore Looks to Cap Successful Year."

29   One of the players who wasn't . . . guard Bill "Foggy" Basham.": Sorrels and Cavagnaro, p. 208.

29   he hitchhiked to Houston and arrived shortly before halftime.: Sorrels and Cavagnaro, pp. 208-09.

29   The guard wouldn't let him in . . . around outside the stadium.: Sorrels and Cavagnaro, p. 209.

29   Six Ole Miss linemen were injured . . . of football in his life.": Sorrels and Cavagnaro, p. 209.

30   "After he got hurt, all Chucky . . . He kept fighting.": Rick Cleveland, "Chucky Mullins -- 20 Years Later: What Is His Legacy?" *The Clarion-Ledger*, Sept. 30, 2009, http://blogs.clarionledger.com/um/2010/09/16/ from-the-archives-chucky-mullins-legacy-at-ole-miss.

30   114 days in a Memphis hospital . . .involved in the fateful play.: Watkins, *Mississippi Football Vault*, p. 109.

30   calling the patch a symbol . . . but how we are to act.: Cleveland, "Chucky Mullins."

30   Chucky Mullins epitomized courage against all odds.: Cleveland, "Chucky Mullins."

31   "Once the game turned in our favor, it kind of snowballed,": Robert Falkoff, "Ole Miss Shows No Mercy to LSU," *The Clarion-Ledger*, April 15, 2001, p. D1, https://secure.pqarchiver.com/clarionledger/ access/2383333581.html.

31   the Tiger head coach finally . . . pitcher to finish up.: Falkoff, "Ole Miss Shows No Mercy to LSU."

32   "When the train was boarded . . . going to be thoroughly tested.": Watkins, *Mississippi Football Vault*, p. 12.

32   "The Center was said to be . . . school and college teams.": Sorrels and Cavagnaro, p. 20.

32   A good contingent of fans . . . bookstore with a telegraph.: Watkins, *Mississippi Football Vault*, p. 12.

32   a couple of Memphis . . . at stealing their signals.: Sorrels and Cavagnaro, p. 22.

32   There was one dominant . . . 'We must beat them.': Watkins, *Mississippi Football Vault*, p. 12.

33   "I learned new words this week," . . . "I needed a dictionary.: Rick Cleveland, "Abysmal? Defense Earns New Adjectives," *Rebel Run: Ole Miss' Magical Season of 2003* (Jackson: The Clarion-Ledger/Sports Publishing L.L.C., 2004), p. 66.

33   "We read and heard all . . . we grew up out there today." Cleveland, "Abysmal?"

33   For whatever reason, we were just sleeping. We woke up today.: Michael Wallace, "No Croc! Rebs Tank Gators 20-17, *Rebel Run: Ole Miss' Magical Season of 2003* (Jackson: The Clarion-Ledger/Sports Publishing L.L.C., 2004), p. 68.

34   the Rebels were a "team . . . Miracle on the Hardwood.": Jerry Porter, "It's a Miracle! Ole Miss to the NCAA," *The Clarion-Ledger*, March 7, 1981, http://www.olemisssports.com/sports/m-baskbl/spec-rel/022009aaa.html.

34   the 68th birthday of Weltlich's father.: Porter, "It's a Miracle!"

35   He told Conerly, who was 24, . . . to a fine senior year,": Sorrels and Cavagnaro, p. 142.

35   Athletic director Tad Smith realized . . . leadership courses to get out.: Sorrels and Cavagnaro, p. 143.

36   "I didn't see that one coming,": "No. 25 Mississippi Hammers Rival 45-0 in Egg Bowl," *Sporting News*, Nov. 28, 2008, http://aol.sportingnews.com/ ncaa-football/story/2008-11-28/no-25-mississippi-hammers-rival.

36   the juggernaut State ran into was primarily the defense.: "No. 25 Mississippi Hammers Rival."

36   Jerry said he never felt . . . to make them pay,": "No. 25 Mississippi Hammers Rival."

36   "We wanted to send a message,": "No. 25 Mississippi Hammers Rival."

36   Total domination.: "No. 25 Mississippi Hammers Rival."

37   "I've never seen a bunch of . . . Man, that game hurt.": Watkins, *Mississippi Football Vault*, p. 65.

37   sentiment arose across the South for a rematch.: Sorrels and Cavagnaro, p. 207.

37   "hit Cannon every time he moved that day,": Watkins, *Mississippi Football Vault*, p. 66.

37   It was unbelievable. Everything was working.: Sorrels and Cavagnaro, p. 207.

38   Ole Miss captain Webster Burke, . . . attempt of the season.: Barner, p. 74.

38   It was the only extra point he ever made in college.: Sorrels and Cavagnaro, p. 92.

38   a good rush from the . . . to pull down the goalposts.: Barner, p. 74.

38   "that was entirely the wrong . . . "including cane-bottom chairs.": Barner, p. xix.

38   players on both sides stayed out of the melee.: Barner, p. 74.

38   shocked officials from both schools . . . the winner footing the bill.: William W. Sorrels, *The Maroon Bulldogs*

REBELS

(Huntsville, AL: The Strode Publishers, Inc., 1975), pp. 91-92.

38 Late in 1926, student delegations . . . a football-shaped trophy to be presented: Sorrels, p. 92.

38 in a "dignified" post-game ceremony: Barner, p. xx.

38 and held for a year by the winning team.: Sorrels, p. 92.

38 Aggie fans responded to the . . . of staging a free for all.: Barner, 74.

39 "arguably the biggest basket in Ole Miss history.": Robert Falkoff, "Rebs Make Sweet 16," *The Clarion-Ledger*, March 18, 2001, http://www.olemisssports.com/sports/m-baskbl/spec-rel/021609aac.html.

39 "a great college basketball game,": Falkoff, "Rebs Make Sweet 16."

39 a bomb that exploded in Notre Dame's face: Falkoff, "Rebs Make Sweet 16."

39 "The little man did it . . . the one we needed most.": Falkoff, "Rebs Make Sweet 16."

39 They just made more plays at crunch time than we did.: Falkoff, "Rebs Make Sweet 16."

40 Boykin spent much of his . . . three touchdowns all season: Barner, p. 147.

40 On the fifth play of the game . . . "sidewheeling through the line": Barner, p. 147.

40 He broke the SEC record with his sixth score: Barner, p. 148.

40 all of Boykin's scores came on . . . State never adjusted to the change.: Sorrels and Cavagnaro, p. 171.

40 I never did keep count, . . . It kept working.: Sorrels and Cavagnaro, p. 171.

41 "Everybody was questioning . . . to start over (in 1988).": Fitzgerald, p. 134.

41 After the game, Ole Miss . . . soak up the celebration mood.: Fitzgerald, p. 134.

42 The Rebels jumped out to a . . . with only two seconds left,: Lee Baker, "Turner Hits Clutcher as Rebs Nip Tigers," *Jackson Daily News*, March 1, 1969, http://www.olemisssports.com/sports/m-baskbl/spec-rel/021409aab.html.

42 he hadn't practiced a lick . . . been sidelined by an illness.: Baker, "Turner Hits Clutcher."

43 After his first talk with the . . . committee reviewed fifty coaches: Sorrels and Cavagnaro, p. 121.

43 He had to take the shortage of . . . the Notre Dame box offense: Sorrels and Cavagnaro, p. 123.

43 LSU doesn't have "anything over . . . to make the best of it.": Sorrels and Cavagnaro, p. 123.

43 I truly wish I had a . . . ahead of LSU, 7 to 0.: Sorrels and Cavagnaro, p. 124.

44 "I'm not going to give up now. I went too far,": Steve Megargee, "Powe's Emergence Proves Patience Pays," *rivals.com*, Sept. 2, 2009, http://collegefootball.rivals.com/content/asp?CID=983095.

44 Every now and then, . . . a lot of heartbreak.: Megargee, "Powe's Emergence."

45 The so-called experts said . . . their status as an also-ran.: Sorrels and Cavagnaro, p. 157.

45 When he took over as . . . Charley Conerly's special talents,: Sorrels and Cavagnaro, p. 157.

45 The offense was perfect for . . . small and undermanned linemen.: Sorrels and Cavagnaro, p. 157.

45 Farley "Fish" Salmon wasn't even . . . decided to give it a shot.: Sorrels and Cavagnaro, p. 157.

45 "Coach Vaught never could accept the fact I was the No. 1 quarterback,": Sorrels and Cavagnaro, p. 157.

45 Even after Salmon won the job . . . to third team in the fall.: Sorrels and Cavagnaro, p. 158.

45 His speed, plus that of . . . small, quick linemen up front.: Sorrels and Cavagnaro, p. 158.

46 before the game, Ross told her,": we've always lost,": Graham Hays, "Rebels Get Defensive, Knock Off Defending Champs," *ESPN.com*, March 20, 2007, http://sports.espn.go/ncw/ncaatourney07/columns/story?columnist=hays_graham.

46 "Mississippi put on a defensive . . . Ole Miss led 35-12.: Hays, "Rebels Get Defensive."

46 "We jumped them, we throttled them.": Hays, "Rebels Get Defensive."

47 rumors swirled that head coach . . . to learn the players' names: Watkins, *Mississippi Football Vault*, p. 122.

47 His situation was complicated . . . well enough to join the team.: Fitzgerald, p. 156.

47 Aware of their new coach's . .the usual ice-cold liquid.: Fitzgerald, pp. 156, 159.

47 I've never been so proud of a football team as I am of you guys tonight.: Fitzgerald, p. 156.

47 "despicable, vile, unprincipled scoundrels.": MacArthur, p. 152.

48 Their father insisted their time . . . always listened on the radio.: "Gigantic Jerrys Excel at Ole Miss," *Sporting News*, Oct. 18, 2007, http://aol.sportingnews.com/ncaa-football/story/2007-10-18/gigantic-jerrys-excel-ole-miss."

48 the result of tossing hay bales . . . sit there and laugh,": "Gigantic Jerrys Excel at Ole Miss."

48 telling her while they . . . be able to sit down,": Gigantic Jerrys Excel at Ole Miss."

48 'When I get big, . . . get you ten pair, too.': "Gigantic Jerrys Excel at Ole Miss."

49 "To be frank, it looked like . . . with about five minutes left.": David Brandt, "Rebels Rally to Stun Arkansas," *The Clarion-Ledger*, March 7, 2010, https://securepqarchiver.com/clarionledger/access/1977708851.html.

49 Head coach Andy Kennedy said . . . and rallied to win.: Brandt, "Rebels Rally to Stun Arkansas."

49 "I saw that team that didn't . . . No big secret.": Brandt, "Rebels Rally to Stun Arkansas."

49 We've been behind in . . . we continue to battle.: Brandt, "Rebels Rally to Stun Arkansas."

50 Bondurant realized that he didn't . . . ready for the first game.: Sorrels and Cavagnaro, p. 19.

50 Rhea was an official.: Sorrels and Cavagnaro, p. 18.

51 Think *Happy Days*, Friday . . . to buy adult beverages.: Ron Higgins, "LSU vs. Ole Miss Always Matters," *SECNation*, Nov. 18, 2010, http://www.secdigitalnetwork.com/SECNation/SECTraditions/tabid/1073/Article/216143.

51 What had heretofore been . . . still friends to this day.": Higgins, "LSU vs. Ole Miss Always Matters."

51 Most of the games were played . . . fans here as they do.: Higgins, "LSU vs. Ole Miss Always Matters."

51 We played in a golden era . . . team performance in high regard.: Higgins, "LSU vs. Ole

Miss Always Matters."

52	If the other team doesn't score, you can't lose.: Michael Wallace, "Rebs Nail Share of SEC West," *Rebel Run: Ole Miss' Magical Season of 2003*, (Jackson: The Clarion-Ledger/Sports Publishing L.L.C., 2004). p. 136.
52	"Our defense played as good as it could play,": Wallace, "Rebs Nail Share of SEC West," p. 136.
52	State's six possessions of the half . . . by linebacker Rob Robertson.: Wallace, "Rebs Nail Share of SEC West," p. 140.
52	The Dog signal caller . . . that missed intended receivers.: Wallace, "Rebs Nail Share of SEC West," p. 141.
52	"I'd have to check . . . best game of the season.": Wallace, "Rebs Nail Share of SEC West," p. 141.
52	With nine minutes left to play . . . a season of abject misery": Rick Cleveland, "Goose Egg Fairly Shouts of Rebs' Rule, Dogs' Despair," *Rebel Run: Ole Miss' Magical Season of 2003*, (Jackson: The Clarion-Ledger/ Sports Publishing L.L.C., 2004). p. 138.
53	"perhaps the greatest tackle in football history.": Sorrels and Cavagnaro, p. 119.
53	his head coach, Ed Walker, claimed . . . He didn't need one.: Sorrels and Cavagnaro, p. 114.
53	In a service football game . . . They backed off.: Sorrels and Cavagnaro, p. 117.
53	In the loss to State in 1936, . . . I don't regret it.": Sorrels and Cavagnaro, p. 119.
54	Freshman quarterback Archie Manning dubbed . . . I wasn't more than 156.": Watkins, *Mississippi Football Vault*, p. 80.
54	recalled watching the Alabama . . . turned Manning loose on them,: Watkins, *Mississippi Football Vault*, p. 80.
54	when the freshman arrived, . . . if they lost to State.: Watkins, *Mississippi Football Vault*, p. 81.
54	No way we were losing that game.: Watkins, *Mississippi Football Vault*, p. 81.
55	Rebel volleyball coach Joe Getzin . . . my eye with her athleticism,": John Holt, "Volleyball's Thomas, an All-American," *The Daily Mississippian*, Jan. 16, 2011, http://www.thedmonline.com/article/volleyballs-thomas-all-american.
55	the kind "of a kid that would do anything to win,": Holt, "Volleyball's Thomas, an All-American."
55	she and her teammates even . . . deserve our own theme song.": Kirby Barkley, "Work Ethic Key for Volleyball's Regina Thomas," *The Daily Mississippian*, Sept. 21, 2010, http://www.thedmonline.com/article/work-ethic-key-volleyballs-regina-thomas.
55	We are just really hard workers.: Barkley, "Work Ethic Key for Volleyball's Regina Thomas."
56	"It was a time," . . . brought up support for football.": Sorrels and Cavagnaro, p. 72.
56	Head coach Bill Driver decided . . . and sent them to Hattiesburg: Watkins, *Mississippi Football Vault*, p. 19.
57	"We can build on this,": "Snead, Ole Miss Stun No. 4 Florida 31-30," *Sporting News*, Sept. 27, 2008, http://aol.sportingnews.com/ncaa-football/story-2008-ole-miss-stun-no-4-florida.
57	"When I crossed the line, . . . going to get the block.": "Snead, Ole Miss Stun No. 4 Florida 31-30."
57	They cavorted with the band and were raucous in the locker room.: "Smiles Linger as Mississippi Looks Ahead to S.C.," *Sporting News*, Sept. 29, 2008, http://aol.sportingnews.com/ncaa-football/story/2008 -09-29/smiles-linger-as-Mississippi-looks-ahead.
57	During the dousing of the coach . . . leaving him with a bloody nose.: "Smiles Linger."
57	They've got to get better . . . get a lot of practice.: "Smiles Linger."
58	in June before the season even . . . The Rebs accepted.: Watkins, *Mississippi Football Vault*, p. 51.
58	So the players watched lesser . . . if they didn't get their suits,: Sorrels and Cavagnaro, p. 150.
58	Vaught intervened and ended that notion.: Sorrels and Cavagnaro, pp. 150-51.
58	We might as well win.: Sorrels and Cavagnaro, p. 151.
59	"Ole Miss was just horrible," . . . I needed the numbers.": Ron Higgins, "Tuohy Can Still Dish," *SECNation*, Jan. 27, 2011, http://www.secdigitalnetwork.com/SECNation/SECTraditions/tabid/1073/Article/219710.
59	When I got [to Ole Miss], . . . court and keep me there.: Higgins, "Tuohy Can Still Dish."
60	It was dubbed "the Stand,": Barner, pp. 280-81.
60	Ole Miss fans assaulted the goalposts.: Fitzgerald, p. 143.
60	I've never seen an effort like that by the guys in red shirts.: Fitzgerald, p. 143.
61	One newspaper called it "The Goof That Laid the Golden Egg.": Barner, p. 177.
61	In the huddle, they had called . . . to see what he could get.: Barner, p. 177.
61	I missed the handoff.: Watkins, *Mississippi Football Vault*, p. 78.
62	an "obituary" since it snapped . . . Alumni were grumbling.: Sorrels and Cavagnaro, p. 282.
62	early in 1973, reports of dissension on the team surfaced.: Sorrels and Cavagnaro, p. 283.
62	After a 17-3 loss to . . . ought to get back in.": Sorrels and Cavagnaro, p. 284.
62	Word of the effort to lure . . . reverberated across campus.: Sorrels and Cavagnaro, pp. 284-85.
62	A delegation approached Vaught . . . do anything for it once.": Sorrels and Cavagnaro, p. 285.
62	Only hours later he met with . . . received a standing ovation.: Sorrels and Cavagnaro, p. 286.
62	It was like Santa Claua . . . were a lot of wet eyes.: Sorrels and Cavagnaro, pp. 286-87.
63	One writer noted that prior . . . and the WNBA scouts.: David Brandt, "No Doubting Rebels' Ignitable Thomas," *The Clarion-Ledger*, Jan. 21, 2010, https://secure.pqarchiver.com/clarionledger/access/1944271281.html.
63	"I've never seen anything quite . . . hit shot after shot.: Brandt, "No Doubting Rebels' Ignitable Thomas."
63	"She's always been quiet," . . . it's speaking very loudly.": Brandt, "No Doubting Rebels' Ignitable Thomas."
63	I can't understand why . . . has everyone's attention now.": Brandt, "No Doubting Rebels' Ignitable Thomas."
64	He spent his early years . . . "You look just like a tadpole.": Sorrels and Cavagnaro, p. 86.
64	Smith spent the summer of . . . drove him to Oxford: Sorrels and Cavagnaro, p. 84.
64	Smith combined exceptional speed . . . would slow him down.: Sorrels and Cavagnaro, p. 86.

206

64 "he brought the physical facilities out of the dark ages.": Sorrels and Cavagnaro, p. 87.

65 a fight broke out between . . . rooms at different times.: Barner, p. 302.

65 each team blamed the other for starting the spat.: Watkins, *Mississippi Football Vault*, p. 119.

65 Stewart Patridge's daily exercise . . . wet ball some at practice.: Barner, p. 302.

65 The head coach knew that . . . their tanks were running low.: Barner, p. 301.

65 Wide receiver Cory Peterson ran a . . . just beyond the goal line,: Watkins, *Mississippi Football Vault*, p. 120.

65 "It was the biggest play of Stew's life and maybe all of our lives," Fitzgerald, p. 150.

65 I changed my mind twice, . . . to go for two.: Fitzgerald, p. 150.

66 "a dismal, drizmal day more fitten for beast than man.: Sorrels and Cavagnaro, p. 201.

66 he sent Flowers to the . . . you're in here with me.": Sorrels and Cavagnaro, p. 201.

67 Even the Ole Miss head coach called the win "miraculous.": Rick Cleveland, "Comeback Victory for the Rebels in the Superdome in 1981," *The Clarion-Ledger*, http://www.olemisssports.com/sports/m-footbl/spec-rel/091010aaa.html.

67 "I've never seen anything . . . that took out of ours,": Cleveland, "Comeback Victory for the Rebels."

67 sidelined with a shoulder injury.: Cleveland, "Comeback Victory for the Rebels."

67 "All seemed so very hopeless for Ole Miss.": Cleveland, "Comeback Victory for the Rebels."

67 Rebs called for a simple . . . away from a Tulane cornerback: Cleveland, "Comeback Victory for the Rebels."

68 "comparisons with his father . . . he would not be coming to Knoxville.: Ian Thomsen, "Out of the Shadows," *Sports Illustrated*, Nov. 12, 2001, http://sportsillustrated.cnn.com/vault/article/magazine/MAG1024250/index.htm.

68 Manning had narrowed his choices down to Texas and Virginia.: Thomsen, "Out of the Shadows."

68 Rebel head coach Tommy . . . wasn't recruiting him harder.": " Watkins, *Mississippi Football Vault*, p. 122.

68 One of the new coach's first priorities was a visit to the Manning home.: Watkins, *Mississippi Football Vault*, p. 122.

69 "the first graduate of . . . a major college scholarship.": John Vaught, *Rebel Coach* (Memphis: Memphis State University Press, 1971), p. 100.

69 "I really wanted to go to . . . Ole Miss and was impressed.: Vaught, *Rebel Coach*, p. 100.

69 Chalk one up for our family affair.: Vaught, *Rebel Coach*, p. 100.

70 "the most significant victory ever recorded: Sorrels and Cavagnaro, p. 177.

70 coach Johnny Vaught called in . . . the rest of the team.: Sorrels and Cavagnaro, p. 172.

70 Vaught began preparing for . . . "the boring ritual paid off.": Sorrels and Cavagnaro, p. 173.

70 They realized that before . . . determine how it set up.: Sorrels and Cavagnaro, pp. 173-74.

70 Vaught used that knowledge . . . on both sides of the ball.: Sorrels and Cavagnaro, p. 173.

70 that made *Newsweek* magazine . . . of the year in all sports.: Sorrels and Cavagnaro, p. 177.

70 Finally it came through.: Sorrels and Cavagnaro, p. 173.

71 Forty minutes of steady screams.": Kareem Copeland, "Rebels Feed Off Energy in Tad Pad," *The Clarion-Ledger*, March 20, 2010, https://secure.pqarchiver.com/clarionledger/access/1988174961.html.

71 Blue-clad Memphis fans . . . team was winning the game.: Copeland, "Rebels Feed Off Energy."

71 "Certainly the emotion was . . . energy off of the crowd.": Copeland, "Rebels Feed Off Energy."

71 Memphis turned the ball . . . on the other end.: Copeland, "Rebels Feed Off Energy."

71 Murphy Holloway and Terrico White . . . of thundering alley-oop dunks.: Copeland, "Rebels Feed Off Energy."

71 When you have a crowd . . . someone other than yourself.: Copeland, "Rebels Feed Off Energy."

72 The students demanded more . . . up with was "empty hands.": Sorrels and Cavagnaro, p. 36.

72 The *Clarion* reported that . . . No doubt they will do it.": Sorrels and Cavagnaro, p. 27.

72 team manager William Cook had trouble . . . for a team in 1895.: Sorrels and Cavagnaro, p. 37.

72 "No one seemed to care . . . kill football in any college,": Sorrels and Cavagnaro, pp. 36-37.

72 student interest suddenly rekindled. . . . to keep the program alive.: Sorrels and Cavagnaro, p. 37.

72 For awhile, the outlook for . . . was very gloomy.: Sorrels and Cavagnaro, p. 36.

73 he worried whether they could keep . . . handle the pressure of the game.: Butch John, "Rebels Upset Vols," *The Clarion-Ledger*, Nov. 12, 2010, http://www.olemisssports.com/sports/m-footbl/spec-rel/111210aaa.html.

73 he prayed.: John, "Rebels Upset Vols."

74 "It was a cow pasture," . . . put our basketball goal.": Dan Fleser, "Gillom's Game Grew Up in Makeshift Setting," *Knoxville News Sentinel*, June 9, 2009, http://knoxnews.com/news/2009/jun//09/gillom-a-real-standout-in-her-field.

74 The competition was mostly . . . black from the dirt,": Fleser, "Gillom's Game Grew Up."

74 We didn't realize we were . . . in Madison Square Garden.: Fleser, "Gillom's Game Grew Up."

75 Coach R.L. Sullivan gave each . . . passengers promptly got seasick.: Sorrels and Cavagnaro, p. 78.

75 "It was a lovely trip. . . . We were supreme people.": Sorrels and Cavagnaro, p. 79.

75 "The Cubans took us all . . . Game day was sunny and warm,: Sorrels and Cavagnaro, p. 79.

75 "but they didn't let them . . . in English to the Mississippians.: Sorrels and Cavagnaro, p. 79.

76 "two quarters of mud wrestling.": Barner, p. 194.

76 "half of Scott Field was . . . a slippery, sloppy mess.": Barner, p. 192.

76 A pregame torrential rain evolved into an afternoon of showers: Barner, p. 193.

76 Both head coaches agreed . . . Numbers were practically illegible.": Barner, p. 192.

76 with lightning flashing all morning long,: Barner pp. 192-93.

76   The smallest crowd in twenty-two years: Barner, p. 193.

76   "a battle royal.": Barner, p. 193.

77   Reese was a really good . . . hadn't jumped in two years.: David Brandt, "The Natural," *The Clarion-Ledger*, May 2, 2008, p. C1, https://secure.pqarchiver.com/clarionledger/access/1740318031.html.

77   "She looked like she might . . . the girl just blew up.": Brandt, "The Natural."

77   I can dunk.: Brandt, "The Natural."

78   "Ole Miss offered a coaching challenge,": Watkins, *Mississippi Football Vault*, p. 49.

78   "When I shook [athletic . . . put out of my mind,": Watkins, *Mississippi Football Vault*, p. 50.

78   he "was a Texan in the . . . out football staff meetings,": Watkins, *Mississippi Football Vault*, p. 49.

78   The heart and soul of Vaught's . . . playing with home-grown talent.: "Mississippi: 1949-57 Ole Miss Rebels," *helmethut.com*, http://www.helmethut.com/College/Ole%20Miss/MSXXUM4957.html.

78   He didn't get the job . . . with two possible recruits." Sorrels and Cavagnaro, p. 140.

78   "no SEC or national championship . . . first factoring in Ole Miss.": "Mississippi: 1949-57 Ole Miss Rebels."

78   I knew Ole Miss could win with its share of Mississippi boys.: Watkins, *Mississippi Football Vault*, p. 49.

79   In 1968, he was 10 years old . . . and his dad in 1977 and '78,: Rusty Hampton, "For 'Rebulldog' Tyler, Rivalry Not Bitter," *The Clarion-Ledger*, Aug, 24, 2003, http://orig.clarionledger.com/news/sports/football2003tab/zrusty.html.

79   "When I ran out on that . . . a Mississippi State helmet.: Hampton, "For 'Rebulldog' Tyler."

79   "It's the people and the . . . up and off the field.: Hampton, "For 'Rebulldog' Tyler."

79   You're not going to get that out of me.: Hampton, "For 'Rebulldog' Tyler."

80   The first time he met with . . . in a bowl game that year.: "Nutt Turns Around No. 20 Ole Miss -- With a Smile," *Sporting News*, Dec. 30, 2008, http://aol.sportingnews.com/ncaa-football/story/2008-12-30/nutt-turns-around-no-20-ole-miss.

80   When Nutt and his staff . . . four straight losing seasons.": "Nutt Turns Around No. 20 Ole Miss."

80   On the practice field and . . . and now it's day,": "Nutt Turns Around No. 20 Ole Miss."

80   "It seems like we've got the . . . deeper rooted than I thought.": "Nutt Turns Around No. 20 Ole Miss."

80   "God put [Nutt] into our . . . experience with these coaches.": "Nutt Turns Around No. 20 Ole Miss."

80   Everybody's positive, every single person on this staff.: "Nutt Turns Around No. 20 Ole Miss."

80   he had never seen Warren . . . and the dramatic knee bend.: Kyle Veazey, "Warren's Free-Throw Shooting Wizardry Nothing Short of Amazing," *The Clarion-Ledger*, March 5, 2011, https://secure.pqarchiver.com/clarionledger/access/2283658561.html.

81   When he gets on the . . . expects it to go in.: Veazey, "Warren's Free-Throw Shooting Wizardry."

82   with 2:42 left in the first quarter, . . . keeping up with each other,: Ron Higgins, "A Strange But Fitting Friendship," *SECNation*, Oct. 28, 2010, http://www.secdigitalnetwork.com/SECNation/SECTraditions/tabid/1073/Article/214902.

82   It is kind of weird, . . . who basically saved my life.: Higgins, "A Strange But Fitting Friendship."

83   In the wake of the unprecedented . . . to be properly identified.": Sorrels and Cavagnaro, p. 107.

83   He asked sports editors . . . more than six hundred suggestions,: Watkins, *Mississippi Football Vault*, p. 36.

83   including Raiders, Confederates, Stonewalls, and simply Ole Miss.: Sorrels and Cavagnaro, p. 109.

83   History credits alumnus Ben Guider as . . . known as the Ole Miss Rebels,: Sorrels and Cavagnaro, p. 109.

84   The Rebels had moved . . . Losing never crossed our mind.: Sorrels and Cavagnaro, p. 203.

85   "It takes 44 pretty good . . . both offense and defense.: Vaught, *Rebel Coach*, p. 72.

85   "Ole Miss players were having children . . . up hurt that togetherness.: Vaught, *Rebel Coach*, p. 74.

85   After the 1950 season, . . . on the road to better football.: Vaught, *Rebel Coach*, p. 75.

85   He decided he didn't have . . . have liked it either.: Vaught, *Rebel Coach*, p. 72.

85   It was the only time I seriously considered leaving Ole Miss.: Vaught, *Rebel Coach*, p. 72.

86   "Laughter is part of the Mississippi mystique.": Vaught, *Rebel Coach*, p. 151.

86   during preparations for the . . . on the traveling squad.: Vaught, *Rebel Coach*, pp. 149-50.

86   They gave him money . . . and threw him into the whirlpool.: Vaught, *Rebel Coach*, p. 152.

86   the players gave him the . . . promptly threw him into the water.: Vaught, *Rebel Coach*, p. 152.

86   he had to be firm and fair but didn't believe in starched collars.: Vaught, *Rebel Coach*, p. 150.

86   In El Paso for the '67 Sun Bowl, . . . realized he had been had.: Vaught, *Rebel Coach*, p. 151.

86   A laugh is better than . . . or a game is close.: Vaught, *Rebel Coach*, p. 149.

87   which boasted a population of 1,100: Fitzgerald, p. 34.

87   One afternoon, a coach from Natchez . . . do almost as I pleased,": Fitzgerald, p. 36.

87   The squatter got evicted, though, . . . a room over an old drug store.: Fitzgerald, p. 38.

88   what the *Memphis Commercial Appeal* called 9:27 of "football hysteria.": Barner, p. 207.

89   Bear Bryant stated he . . . with freshmen could beat me.": Sorrels and Cavagnaro, p. 169.

89   "Ole Miss simply was not ready . . . reported in the fall of 1949.: Sorrels and Cavagnaro, p. 163.

89   The coaches made sure the . . . Bryant's remark to memory.: Sorrels and Cavagnaro, p. 169.

89   Kentucky appeared to have saved . . . said Kentucky had won 23-21.: Sorrels and Cavagnaro, p. 169.

90   joined Cheryl Miller as the only . . . 400 assists, and 400 steals.: "Armintie Price," *OleMissSports.com*, http://www.olemisssports.com/sports/w-baskbl/mtt/price_armintie00.html.

90   "My mom was my life," . . . doesn't feel weird to me,": Dick Patrick, "Price's Relentless Hustle Inspiring for Ole Miss," *USA Today*, March 14, 2007, http://www.usatoday.com/sports/college/womensbasketball/dayton/2007-03-13.

90   I talk to God and Mom and ask for guidance and help.: Patrick, "Price's Relentless Hustle."

91   He had discovered football . . . in the early autumn of 1893,: Watkins, *Mississippi Football Vault*, p. 7.
91   the thin, moustachioed, 28-year-old: Sorrels and Cavagnaro, p. 11.
91   presented the idea of a university . . . to forge ahead with a team.: Watkins, *Mississippi Football Vault*, p. 7.
91   A few days later, at 6:30 a.m. . . . led them on a four-mile run.: Sorrels and Cavagnaro, p. 11.
91   "It shocked the conservatism of many . . . through the streets of the town.": Sorrels and Cavagnaro, p. 13.
91   Not a single student finished . . . "Bondurant's fool football team.": Sorrels and Cavagnaro, p. 11.
91   The next morning, though, twenty students returned.: Sorrels and Cavagnaro, pp. 11-12.
91   Senior law student Alfred Holt . . . on another four-mile run.: Sorrels and Cavagnaro, p. 12.
92   We don't care about the glory. We want wins.": Rick Cleveland, "Offensive Linemen Pave Way to Win,"
         Rebel Run: Ole Miss' Magical Season of 2003, (Jackson: *The Clarion-Ledger*/Sports Publishing L.L.C.,
         2004), p. 110.
92   routed the South Carolina Gamecocks for 43 minutes.: Cleveland, "Offensive Linemen Pave Way to Win."
92   seven-man rotation in the . . . and lost their focus.: Cleveland, "Offensive Linemen Pave Way to Win."
92   Carolina had a pair of . . . to stop the run.: Cleveland, "Offensive Linemen Pave Way to Win."
93   Auburn led 25-13 in the last . . . to a stirring comeback: "100 Years Flashback: 1928 Southern Conference
         Tournament Champions," *OleMissSports.com*, Dec. 10, 2008, http://www.olemisssports.com/sport/m-
         baskbl/spec-rel/121008aab.html.
93   Many of the spectators . . . so as not to be humiliated.: "100 Years Flashback: 1928 Southern Conference
         Tournament Champions."
94   Ole Miss' battle against Tennessee . . . with Archie Manning's arm.: Watkins, *Mississippi Football Vault*,
         pp. 90-91.
94   When a writer suggested that . . . "I think they have mules,": Sorrels and Cavagnaro, p. 265.
94   Aware of the danger of giving . . . The player refused.: Sorrels and Cavagnaro, pp. 265-66.
94   His ill-conceived words were . . . Rebels were frothing.": Watkins, *Mississippi Football Vault*, p. 91.
94   "the campus and an entire . . . "Squeeze the Orange" sign.: Sorrels and Cavagnaro, p. 266.
94   The capacity crowd "stared in disbelief at the ease of the Rebel score.": Sorrels and Cavagnaro, p. 268.
94   Middle guard Larry Thomas led . . . team effort I've ever witnessed.": Watkins, *Mississippi Football Vault*,
         p. 91.
94   Manning declared Ole Miss . . . we proved it today,": Watkins, *Mississippi Football Vault*, p. 91.
94   Sophomore Randy Reed got in . . . really is a big mouth.": Watkins, *Mississippi Football Vault*, p. 92.
94   Man, we're gonna kill them for what they've said.: Sorrels and Cavagnaro, p. 265.
95   My luck ain't going too good right now.": "Ole Miss DE Greg Hardy Eases into Final Season," *Sporting News*,
         Aug. 14, 2009, http://aol.sportingnews.com/ncaa-football/story/2009-08-14/ole-miss-de-greg-hardy-
         eases-into-final-season.
95   Old questions about his . . . not his mind but his foot.: "Ole Miss DE Greg Hardy."
96   He even turned down . . . preparing for the next game.: Sorrels and Cavagnaro, p. 139.
96   At TCU, Vaught played for . . . coach's tires in retaliation.: Sorrels and Cavagnaro, p. 138.
96   He wanted his scouts to . . . had in his shoelaces.: Sorrels and Cavagnaro, p. 136.
96   In 1946, Bryant's defense had . . . made their last move.: Sorrels and Cavagnaro, p. 144.
96   outgained the Cats 233-166, . . . George Lambert, and Everette Harper.: Watkins, *Mississippi Football Vault*,
         p. 53.
96   [Johnny] Vaught was at his best in preparation.: Sorrels and Cavagnaro, p. 136.
97   What Rebel head baseball coach . . . the 2009 regional championship game.: NCAA: Pomeranz Leads
         Ole Miss Past W. Kentucky 4-1," *Sporting News*, June 2, 2009, http://aol.sportingnews.com/mlb/
         story/2009-06-01/ncaa-pomeranz-leads-ole-miss-past-w-kentucky.
97   "That was a legendary . . . a Curt Schilling-bloody sock moment.": "NCAA: Pomeranz Leads Old Miss."
98   Pope discovered that Miller's kicks . . . and two running backs.: Ron Reed, "Ah! Those Punts Hit the Spot,"
         Sports Illustrated, Oct. 16, 1978, http://sportsillustrated.cnn.com/vault/article/magazine/MAG1094194/
         index.htm.
98   In pregame warmups for the . . . we have to watch him,": Reed, "Ah! Those Punts Hit the Spot."
99   Prior to the 1913 game against . . . Cumberland declined,: Sorrels and Cavagnaro, p. 73.
99   saying the idea was silly.: Watkins, *Mississippi Football Vault*, p. 19.
99   "The teams of the effete . . . to commercialize the sport.": Sorrels and Cavagnaro, p. 73.
99   On Oct. 17, 1914, the Rebels . . . wearing numbered jerseys.: Watkins, *Mississippi Football Vault*, p. 20.
99   In the fall of 1918, head . . . to suit him up.: Sorrels and Cavagnaro, p. 76.
99   When the player walked out . . . this scarecrow come from?": Sorrels and Cavagnaro, pp. 76-77.
99   I cannot agree with coach . . . the aspect of a chain gang.: Sorrels and Cavagnaro, p. 73.
100   Vaught staggered as he was . . . eager to rejoin his team,: Sorrels and Cavagnaro, p. 272.
100   during his second night at . . . intensive care in Memphis.: Sorrels and Cavagnaro, p. 273.
100   As his illness improved, . . . signed a one-year extension.: Sorrels and Cavagnaro, p. 274.
100   in January 1971, Vaught's doctor . . . the man who had hired him: Sorrels and Cavagnaro, p. 275.
100   John, if you can't coach . . . be the athletic director.: Sorrels and Cavagnaro, p. 275.

BIBLIOGRAPHY

"100 Years Flashback: 1928 Southern Conference Tournament Champions." *OleMissSports. com.* 10 Dec. 2008, http://www.olemisssports.com/sports/m-baskbl/spec-rel/ 121008aab.html.

Alford, Parrish. "McFerrin, a Former Tupelo High Star, Lands Starting Role for Ole Miss." *NEMS360.com.* 10 Feb. 2011. http://nems360.com/view/full_story/11339451/article.

Anderson, Kelli. "Rebels with a Cause." *Sports Illustrated.* 20 Jan. 1997. http://sports illustrated.cnn.com/vault/article/magazine/MAG1009379/index.htm.

"Arkansas Fans Greet Nutt with Boos." *Sporting News.* 25 Oct. 2008. http://aol.sportingnews. com/ncaa-football/story/2008-10-25/arkansas-fans-greet-nutt-boos.

"Armintie Price." *OleMissSports.com.* http://www.olemisssports.com/sports/w-baskbl/mtt/ price_armintie00.html.

Baker, Lee. "Turner Hits Clutcher as Rebs Nip Tigers." *Jackson Daily News.* 1 March 1969. http://www.olemisssports.com/sports/m-baskbl/spec-rel/021409aab.html.

Barkley, Kirby. "Work Ethic Key for Volleyball's Regina Thomas." *The Daily Mississippian.* 21 Sept. 2010. http://www.thedmonline.com/article/work-ethic-key-volleyballs-regina-thomas.

Barner, William G. *The Egg Bowl: Mississippi State vs. Ole Miss.* Jackson: University Press of Mississippi, 2007.

Brandt, David. "Grill's New Patience at Plate May Lift UM to NCAA Bid." *The Clarion-Ledger.* 15 April 2010. https://secure.pqarchiver.com/clarionledger/access/2009830301. html.

---. "No Doubting Rebels' Ignitable Thomas." *The Clarion-Ledger.* 21 Jan. 2010. https://secure. pqarchiver.com/clarionledger/access/1944271281.html.

---. "Rebels Rally to Stun Arkansas, Tie Dogs for West Title." *The Clarion-Ledger.* 7 March 2010. https://secure.pqarchiver.com/clarionledger/access/1977708851.html.

---. "The Natural." *The Clarion-Ledger.* 2 May 2008. C1. https://secure.pqarchiver.com/ clarionledger/access/1740318031.html.

Cleveland, Rick. "Abysmal? Defense Earns New Adjectives." *Rebel Run: Ole Miss' Magical Season of 2003.* Jackson: *The Clarion-Ledger*/Sports Publishing L.L.C., 2004. 66.

---. "Chucky Mullins -- 20 Years Later: What Is His Legacy?" *The Clarion-Ledger.* 30 Sept. 2009. http://blogs.clarionledger.com/um/2010/09/16/from-the-archives-chucky-mullins-legacy-at-ole-miss.

---. Comeback Victory for the Rebels in the Superdome in 1981." *The Clarion-Ledger.* http:// www.olemisssports.com/sports/m-footbl/spec-rel/091010aaa.html.

---. "Goose Egg Fairly Shouts of Rebs' Rule, Dogs' Despair." *Rebel Run: Ole Miss' Magical Season of 2003.* Jackson: *The Clarion-Ledger*/Sports Publishing L.L.C., 2004. 138.

---. "Injuries? Noise? Pressure? Rebels Answer the Call." *Rebel Run: Ole Miss' Magical Season of 2003.* Jackson: *The Clarion-Ledger*/Sports Publishing L.L.C., 2004. 118.

---. "Offensive Linemen Pave Way to Win." *Rebel Run: Ole Miss' Magical Season of 2003.* Jackson: *The Clarion-Ledger*/Sports Publishing L.L.C., 2004. 110.

---. "Rebels Beat State in Overtime." *The Clarion-Ledger.* 24 Jan. 1981. http://www.olemiss sports.com/sports/m-baskbl/spec-rel/013009aab.html.

Copeland, Kareem. "Rebels Feed Off Energy in Tad Pad to Bolt Past Tigers, into 3rd Round." *The Clarion-Ledger.* 20 March 2010. https://secure.pqarchiver.com/ clarionledger/access/1988174961.html.

Dubose, Kaitlyn. "McFerrin Walk-On Turned Starter for Lady Rebs." *The Daily Missis-sippian.* 22 Feb. 2011. http://www.thedmonline.com/article/mcferrin-walk-turned-starter-lady-rebs.

Falkoff, Robert. "Ole Miss Shows No Mercy to LSU." *The Clarion-Ledger*. 15 April 2001. D1. https://secure.pqarchiver.com/clarionledger/access/2383333581.html.

---. "Rebs Make Sweet 16." *The Clarion-Ledger*. 18 March 2001. http://www.olemisssports. com/sports/m-baskbl/spec-real/021609aac.html.

Fitzgerald, Francis J., ed. *Greatest Moments in Ole Miss Football History*. Birmingham: Epic Sports, 1999.

Fleser, Dan. "Gillom's Game Grew Up in Makeshaft Setting." *Knoxville News Sentinel*. 9 June 2009. http://www.knoxnews.com/news/2009/jun/09/gillom-a-real-standout-in-her-field.

"Gigantic Jerrys Excel at Ole Miss -- with Assist from Mom." *Sporting News*. 18 Oct. 2007. http://aol.sportingnews.com/ncaa-football/story/2007-10-18/gigantic-jerrys-excel-ole-miss-assist-mom.

Goreham, Janet. "Rebel with a Cause." *Sharing the Victory Magazine*. http://www.sharing thevictory.com/vsItemDisplay.lsp?method=display&objectid=AD9A09.

Hampton, Rusty. "For 'Rebulldog' Tyler, Rivalry Not Bitter." *The Clarion-Ledger*." 24 Aug. 2003. http://orig.clarionledger.com/news/sports/football2003tab/zrusty.html.

Hays, Graham. "Rebels Get Defensive, Knock Off Defending Champs." *ESPN.com*. 20 March 2007. http://sports.espn.go.com/ncw/ncaatourney07/columns/story?columnist=hays_graham.

Higgins, Ron. "A Strange But Fitting Friendship." *SECNation*. 28 Oct. 2010. http://www. secdigitalnetwork.com/SECNation/SECTraditions/tabid/1073/Article/214902.

---. "LSU vs. Ole Miss Always Matters." *SECNation*. 18 Nov. 2010. http://www.secdigitalnet work.com/SECNation/SECTraditions/tabid/1073/Article/216143.

---. "Tuohy Can Still Dish." *SECNation*. Jan. 27, 2011. http://www.secdigitalnetwork/SEC Nation/SECTraditions/tabid/1073/Article/219710.

Holt, John. "Vlaar Mature Beyond Her Years." *The Daily Mississippian*. 9 March 2011. http:// www.thedmonline.com/article/vlaar-mature-beyond-her-years.

---. "Volleyball's Thomas, an All-American." *The Daily Mississippian*. 16 Feb. 2011. http:// www.thedmonline.com/article/volleyballs-thomas-all-american.

John, Butch. "Ole Miss Holds Off Vanderbilt." *The Clarion-Ledger*. 23 Oct. 1983. http://www. olemisssports.com/sports/m-footbl/spec-rel/091710aaa.html.

---. "Rebels Upset Vols." *The Clarion-Ledger*. 12 Nov. 2010. http://www.olemisssports.com/ sports/m-footbl/111210aaa.html.

MacArthur, John. *Twelve Ordinary Men*. Nashville: W Publishing Group, 2002.

Marcello, Brandon. "Quiet Leader Bolden Ready to Take Charge as Senior." *The Clarion-Ledger*. 8 July 2011. http://www.clarionledger.com/article/20220708/SPORTS 030103/107080335.

Megargee, Steve. "Powe's Emergency Proves Patience Pays." *rivals.com*. 2 Sept. 2009. http:// collegefootball.rivals.com/content.asp?CID=983095.

"Mississippi: 1949-57 Ole Miss Rebels." *helmethut.com*. http://www.helmethut.com/College/ Ole%20Miss/MSXXUM4957.html.

"NCAA: Pomeranz Leads Ole Miss Past W. Kentucky 4-1." *Sporting News*. 2 June 2009. http://aol.sportingnews.com/mlb/story/2009-06-01/ncaa-pomeranz-leads-ole-miss-past-w-kentucky.

"No. 25 Mississippi Hammers Rival 45-0 in Egg Bowl." *Sporting News*. 28 Nov. 2008. http:// aol.sportingnews.com/ncaa-football/story/2008-11-28/no-25-mississippi-hammers-rival.

"Nutt Turns Around No. 20 Ole Miss -- With a Smile." *Sporting News*. 30 Dec. 2008. http://aol.sportingnews.com/ncaa-football/story/2008-12-30/nutt-turns-around-no-20.

"Ole Miss DE Greg Hardy Eases into Final Season." *Sporting News*. 14 Aug. 2009. http://aol.sportingnews.com/ncaa-football/story/2009-08-14/ole-miss-de-greg-hardy-eases-into-final-season.

Patrick, Dick. "Price's Relentless Hustle Inspiring for Ole Miss." *USA Today*. 14 March 2007. http://www.usatoday.com/sports/college/womensbasketball/dayton/2007-03-13.

Porter, Jerry. "It's a Miracle! Ole Miss to the NCAA." *The Clarion-Ledger*. 7 March 1981. http://www.olemisssports.com/sports/m-baskbl/spec-rel/022009aaa.html.

"Rebels Hold On in Nutt's Return to Arkansas." *Sporting News*. 25 Oct. 2008. http://aol.sportingnews.com/ncaa-football/story/2008-10-25/rebels-hold-nutts-return-arkansas.

Reed, Ron. "Ah! Those Punts Hit the Spot." *Sports Illustrated*. 16 Oct. 1978. http://sportsillustrated.cnn.com/vault/article/magazine/MAG1094194/index.htm.

Sigler, Matt. "Moore Looks to Cap Successful Year at NCAA Championships." *The Daily Mississippian*. 7 June 2011. http://www.thedmonlin.com/article/moore-looks-cap-successful-year-ncaa-championships.

"Smiles Linger as Mississippi Looks Ahead to S.C." *Sporting News*. 29 Sept. 2008. http://aol.sportingnews.com/ncaa-football/story/2008-09-29/smiles-linger-as-mississippi-looks-ahead-to-sc.

"Snead, McCluster Lead Ole Miss Past Texas Tech." *Sporting News*. 2 Jan. 2009. http://aol.sportingnews.com/ncaa-football/story/2009-01-02/snead-muccluster-lead-ole-miss.

"Snead, Ole Miss Stun No. 4 Florida 31-30." *Sporting News*. 27 Sept. 2008. http://aol.sporting-news.com/ncaa-football/story/2008-09-27/snead-ole-miss-stun-no-4-florida-31-30.

Sorrels, William W. *The Maroon Bulldogs: Mississippi State Football*. Huntsville, AL: The Strode Publishers, Inc., 1975.

Sorrels, William W. and Charles Cavagnaro. *Ole Miss Rebels: Mississippi Football*. Huntsville, AL: The Strode Publishers, Inc., 1976.

Stephens, Derek. "The Story of Brandon Bolden: Proving the Doubters Wrong." *Bleacher Report.com*. 22 April 2009. http://bleacherreport.com/article/160452-the-story-of-brandon-bolden.

"Texas Tech, Ole Miss Meet in Cotton Bowl Farewell." *Sporting News*. 1 Jan. 2009. http://aol.sporting news.com/ncaa-football/story/2009-01-01/texas-tech-ole-miss-meet.

Thomsen, Ian. "Out of the Shadows." *Sports Illustrated*. 12 Nov. 2001. http://sportsillustrated.cnn.com/vault/article/magazine/MAG1024250/index.htm.

Tower, Ivory. "The Grove Bracket: (1) Eli Manning v. (8) Lauren Grill." *RedCupRebellion.com*. 1 June 2010. http://www.redcuprebellion.com/2010/6/1/1454225.

Vaught, John. *Rebel Coach: My Football Family*. Memphis: Memphis State University Press, 1971.

Veazey, Kyle. "Warren's Free-Throw Shooting Wizardry Nothing Short of Amazing." *The Clarion-Ledger*. 5 March 2011. https://secure/pqarchiver.com/clarionledger/access/2283658561.html.

Wallace, Michael. "6-0: Only One to Go; After 24-20 Victory, Just LSU Is Left in Ole Miss' Way." *Rebel Run: Ole Miss' Magical Season of 2003*. Jackson: *The Clarion-Ledger*/Sports Publishing L.L.C., 2004. 116, 119-20.

---. "No Croc! Rebs Tank Gators 20-17." *Rebel Run: Ole Miss' Magical Season of 2003*. Jackson: *The Clarion-Ledger*/Sports Publishing L.L.C., 2004. 64, 67-68.

---. "Rebels Rule in Real World." *The Clarion-Ledger*. 28 Dec. 2002. D1, https://secure.pq archiver.com/clarionledger/access/1834566511.html.

---. "Rebs Nail Share of SEC West." *Rebel Run: Ole Miss' Magical Season of 2003*. Jackson: *The Clarion-Ledger*/Sports Publishing L.L.C., 2004. 136, 139-41.

Watkins, Billy. "Rebels, Mother Nature Stop Bulldogs." *OleMissSports.com*. http://www.olemisssports.com/sports/m-footbl/spec-rel/112808aae.html.

---. *University of Mississippi Football Vault: The History of the Rebels*. Atlanta: Whitman Publishing, LLC, 2009.

REBELS

INDEX
(LAST NAME, DEVOTION DAY NUMBER)

213